£3-50
HRB

Boat
Tuning
for
Speed

Boat Tuning for Speed

Fred Imhoff &
Lex Pranger

Nautical

First published © 1975
by
United Nautical Publishers SA, Basle

This edition published © 1975
by
NAUTICAL PUBLISHING COMPANY Ltd
Nautical House, Lymington, Hampshire, England

in association with
George G. Harrap & Co Ltd,
London

ISBN 0-245.52563.7

Printed in Spain
by
Gráficas Estella, S.A.
Estella (Navarra)
Depósito Legal NA - 653 - 75

Colour separations: Laudert + Co, Vreden, W. Germany

Text setting: BAS Printers Limited, Wallop, England

PREFACE

This book is intended as a manual for the racing and cruising sailor who wants to get more boat-speed or who is trying to solve problems concerning the trim, layout or fitting-out of his boat.

It deals clearly and logically with all aspects of boat tuning. It enables the reader to find the cause or causes of his problems in a practical approach, theory being as far as possible avoided. Instead, illustrations show directly and rapidly what is intended and the advice given is based on actual practice because there is no doubt that real experience is the best teacher.

Every sailor can improve his boat-speed. It is not witchcraft which makes a fast boat. Most problems of tuning have a very simple solution. Even the most talented sailors have had to learn from the beginning the elements which go to make for maximum speed and a perfectly set-up boat. In practice we find that the tuning of a boat is a step-by-step process which follows logical reasoning.

This book is born out of actual experience and is intended as a guide through the labyrinth of possibilities which finally lead to the optimum boat with optimum speed.

To give an example of how to use the book, the problem might be that boat-speed is good but pointing is poor.

We look under the chapter 'Sailing to Windward' and we find the section dealing with 'Windward Ability'. After checking out all the possibilities let us say that we come to the conclusion that the fault lies in too much side-bend in the mast.

Then go to the chapter 'The Mast' and under the section on 'Control of Side-bend' you can find all the methods of reducing sideways bend.

The authors do not pretend to give a completely detailed list in this book of all the factors in the trim, fitting-out or layout of a boat which affect speed. The subject is so very extensive that it is impractical to cover it all and so we have chosen the most important, or most frequently troublesome, points and dealt with these thoroughly.

FRED IMHOFF and LEX PRANGER

Weteringbrug, Holland, 1975

CONTENTS

Part One—HULL and RIG

Chapter 1.
THE HULL

The Surface Finish

The basis of a fast boat is, of course, a good hull. That is to say, a hull which is built to have the most favourable shape within the tolerances, is as stiff as possible and has a perfect surface.

Out of these three speed-making factors the hull surface is of very great importance and its treatment is entirely up to the owner himself.

The total hull resistance can be divided into that which depends on its shape and that which comes from friction. There is not much the owner can do to the hull shape, especially in one-design classes, except to decrease turbulence (see page 5). To keep friction as low as possible one should bear in mind that function should prevail over beauty and so the emphasis should always be on the former.

Take for example a beautifully varnished boat. It will always be at a slight disadvantage against a painted boat, firstly, because the surface can never be as smooth since fillers cannot be used without spoiling the beauty. Secondly, damage and scratches cannot be removed as they can on a paint finish where cement can be trowelled on to level up the surface.

For minimum frictional resistance one needs a hull surface which causes no turbulence whatsoever but to which a thin water-film can remain attached by means of a microscopic roughness. This thin layer ensures that friction only acts through adjacent water layers and is thus at a minimum.

A beautifully painted or sprayed hull with a high gloss will repel water and this causes friction between paint and water which is higher than the friction resulting between adjacent water layers.

It is the same with a glossy fibreglass hull where there is similar friction between the polyester gelcoat and water.

The best practicable surface can easily be obtained by treating the hull, both below and above the water line, with 400 grade waterproof abrasive paper. You should never use car wax or silicone wax or other water repellent finishes on a fast hull.

It is a well known fact that a dolphin is a fast mover and its skin has a surface layer of slime which holds a thin layer of water. Here we see the same effect where the friction is only between adjacent water layers and hence is low.

Furthermore, it is of the utmost importance that the hull surface is absolutely grease-free and you can keep it this way by rubbing very lightly with the same fine waterproof abrasive paper or you can clean the hull with an ordinary clothes washing detergent.

You can check the efficiency of a surface very easily. Throw some water onto the surface and, if drops remain, then it is water repellent. If the water spreads evenly in a microscopically thin film then it is a good surface for speed.

The drawings represent three types of surface, highly magnified, in contact with a moving flow of water.

The top drawing shows a rough surface which results in eddies and turbulence which absorb energy and this results in higher frictional resistance.

The centre drawing shows a smooth but water repellent surface which can occur, not only because of wax or grease, but also because the surface may be simply too smooth. Air bubbles adhering to the surface cause extra turbulence which increases the already high friction between water and hull.

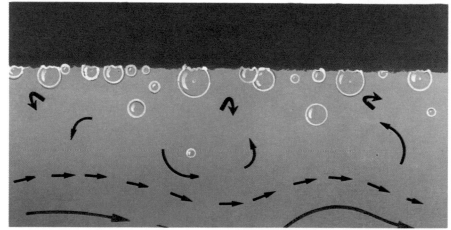

The lower drawing shows an ideal surface in which the small granulations hold a thin water film which becomes almost a part of the hull and is carried along with it. Each microscopic layer of water thereafter moves slightly faster until the full water speed is reached a few millimetres out from the hull. The friction is therefore only between water and water and this is much less than between water and paint.

The ideal surface for small boats has about .005 mm granular roughness and this can be obtained by rubbing down wet with 400 grade abrasive paper.

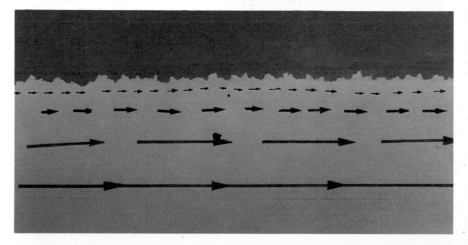

The graph, which is based on large numbers of practical evaluations made in a test tank, represents the differences in frictional resistance (D) between the three typical surfaces just discussed, plotted against hull speed (V/KN).

Curve A represents the rough surface. Curve B shows the smooth polished water resistant surface and curve C the nearly ideal surface with the optimum granular size.

The curves clearly show that, because the resistance increases by the square compared with the speed, the difference is greatly magnified as the speed builds up. Therefore fast boats, especially those which plane, need much the most careful attention.

Do not forget that the whole of the hull, not only the underwater part has to be dealt with. When the boat heels or is crashing through waves, there is running water everywhere on the hull and possibly on the decks also.

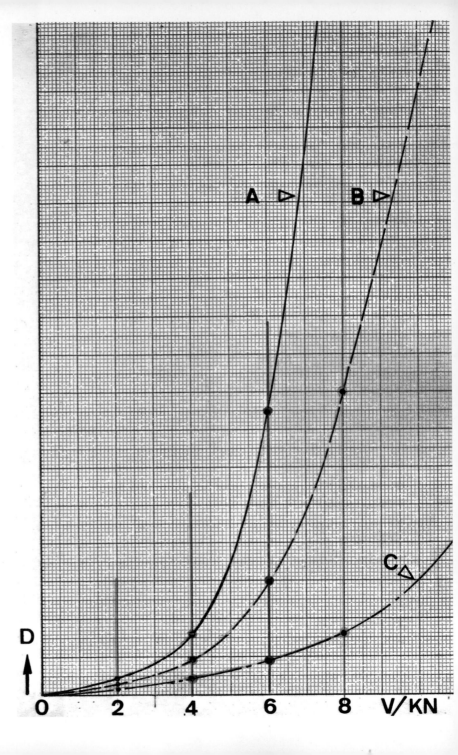

Resistance due to hull shape

The other main ingredient in the overall resistance to forward progress is that caused by the shape of the hull pushing through the water. To most small boat sailors this is of little importance since the boat's shape is fixed and the possibility of altering it is virtually nil. There are, however, some apparently small details which can be attended to with a surprisingly large effect on the overall resistance. Examples are the fairing in of chafing strips, bailers and keelbands. The greatest attention should also be paid to the centreboard slot and its sealing strips.

A common fault is seen in the angle between the boat's bottom and the transom where a small amount of rounding can cause the water to curl round and upwards adding an appreciable amount to the drag (see upper drawing). A wave is then formed behind the transom which is dragged along, absorbs energy and acts as a brake.

Sometimes this rounding off is in the original mould but it can also be caused by the careless use of abrasives in an effort to smooth the bottom, or by damage.

The delivery of the water flow at the edge must be clean and this can only occur if the corner is flat and square. If the rules permit, it is best to insert at the edge a strip of a hard material like stainless steel which can be filed off sharp and flush. The water then has no chance

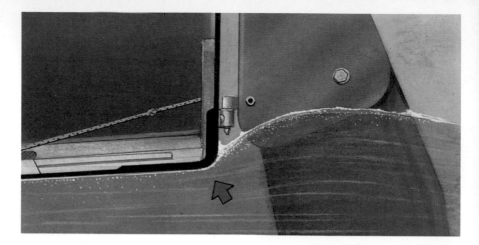

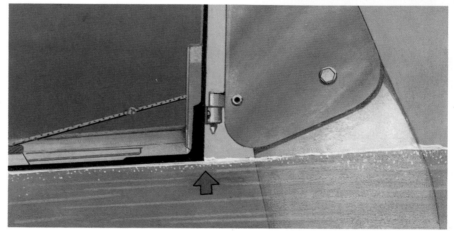

of creeping round the corner but leaves it cleanly resulting in a flat smooth wake. Another bonus is that the rudderhead is kept clear of the water flow.

So it can be definitely stated that there is a real advantage in regular maintenance to such sharp edges which can often suffer minor damage especially on launching.

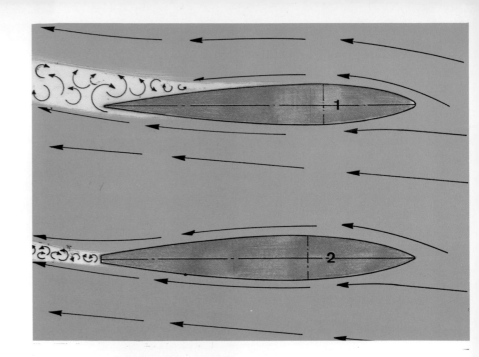

Centreboard and rudder sections

The normal section which is used for centreboards and rudders is something like that shown in drawing No. 1 and has a sharp, finely tapered trailing edge. But a centreboard does not travel straight forward. It moves at a slight angle to the water flow depending on the leeway and this produces turbulence on the low pressure side. A more nearly ideal shape would be asymmetrical, but practical difficulties rule this out.

However, it has been found from recent tests made at the Delft Technical College in Holland that improvement can be obtained by cutting the trailing edge off to a narrow flat about two to three milli-metres wide and with sharp corners. The effect is to hold the attached water flow on the low pressure side so that the breakaway point moves

farther aft. This results in lower friction. Another bonus is that the aft edge is less vulnerable to damage.

The main part of the section is not too critical but the maximum chord should be about one third of the width back from the leading edge and the latter should not be sharp but rounded to a small radius. A parabolic section is ideal.

The rudder section can be the same with the exception that the trailing edge should be as sharp as possible at the waterline.

The principle governing the thickness is that a blade which is set straight into the water flow should be as thin as possible and also, in general, faster speeds need thinner sections. But, centreboards always act at an angle to the flow and move

slowly when the boat is close-hauled and so the maximum thickness allow-ed by the rules is usually best, except for fast catamarans.

Rudders act often at greater angles, especially in rough weather when violent helm movements may be necessary, and so thicker and blunter sections which discourage stalling can prove better.

Since friction is proportional to the pressure on a surface, and because centreboards and rudders work under great pressure, these surfaces need even more careful treatment than the hull.

Colour is also important, white being best, so that weed or dirt can be seen easily. Also, white reflects sunlight, and this minimises the possibility of warping due to heat.

Compare the two drawings on the right in which the upper rudder is of poor design. Note the following points.

The pintle extends below the boat's bottom and the rudderhead itself is set too low. The front and underside of the rudderhead are flat (see right, black arrow). The lower aft corner of the rudderhead is rounded (left, black arrow) and, as with the rounded edge to the transom discussed earlier, a wave can form and be dragged along behind the rudder. The line which hoists the lifting blade is fixed to it below the waterline which adds to the turbulence. The blade section is poor, particularly the aft side near the waterline.

Note how all these points are improved in the lower rudder. The green arrow on the right points to the sharp cut-off on the angle between transom and the boat's bottom. The whole rudderhead is raised clear of the water level (upper green arrow) but, should waves strike it, the streamlining is as good as possible and the after edge is cut off square. The uphaul line is also fixed above water. The trailing edge of the blade is a clean cut-off except at the waterline (lower green arrow).

If class rules allow, it is even better to make the blade, rudderhead and tiller in one piece so that it is as light and rigid as possible with no play anywhere.

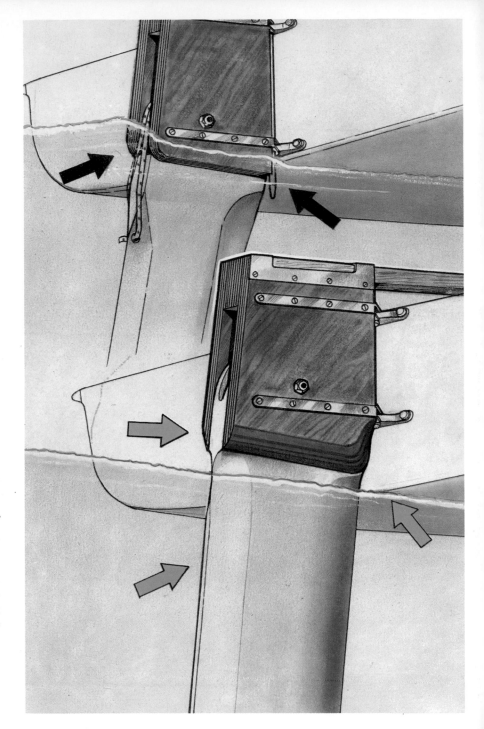

The centreboard case

Not only is the blade section and surface treatment of the centreboard of great importance, but so is the centreboard case and the way it is arranged. In fact a poorly designed case can completely ruin a boat's performance.

A common fault is for the case to be too wide, thus allowing the board to flop from side to side, especially when reaching or running. Helm movements and changes in the wind's pressure can cause the board to rock in its case and the thumps and jerks can be most unsettling to the crew's concentration. The rock also causes turbulence (see drawing) and gives an opportunity for the board to twist, both of which add to the drag. Still more turbulence is caused by water being pumped in and out of the case by the board flopping sideways.

Vibration, especially at speed, can also be caused by a loose fit, though more usually the reason is that the curve of the section is different on one side from the other. Vibration means that the board has a greater effective thickness and hence a greater resistance.

There are several ways of holding the centreboard steady whilst, at the same time, enabling it to be raised and lowered smoothly and with minimum friction. One good method is shown here.

The slots at the top and bottom of the case should be very accurately made and lined with PTFE (Poly-

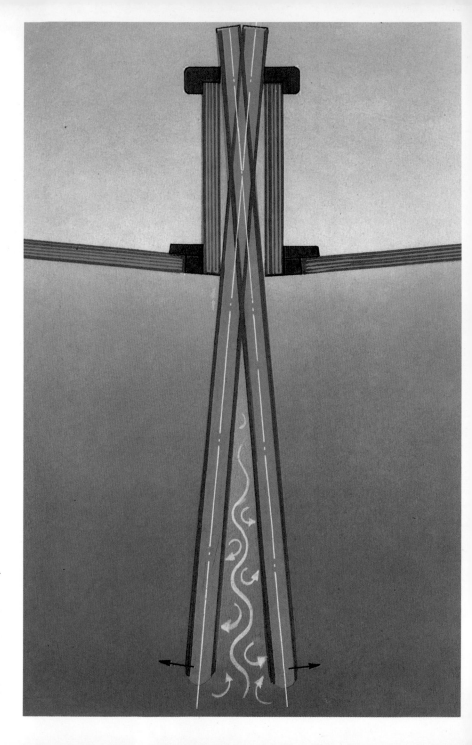

tetra-fluor-ethylene or Teflon), which has a very low coefficient of friction and allows the board to move smoothly even when under side pressure (see arrows). If it is impossible to make the case as shown another suggestion is to build up the part of the centreboard that is in the case with a hard plastic laminate and to line the case with PTFE making it a very close fit.

The disadvantage of this, however, is that sand or dirt can easily scratch the surfaces or even jam the board. Better is to line the case with spaced vertical strips of PTFE which gives clearance for sand to drop out.

The lifting rudder

Some of these faults also apply to the rudder where loose pintles and gudgeons, loose tiller joints at the rudderhead, sloppy fit between rudderhead and blade, and poor section shapes cause difficulty in control, vibration or extra drag.

A lifting rudder can be clamped with a screw and butterfly nut to prevent play between the blade and the head but, since it is seldom of great advantage to lift the blade, it is better to make the rudder all in one piece and forget about it.

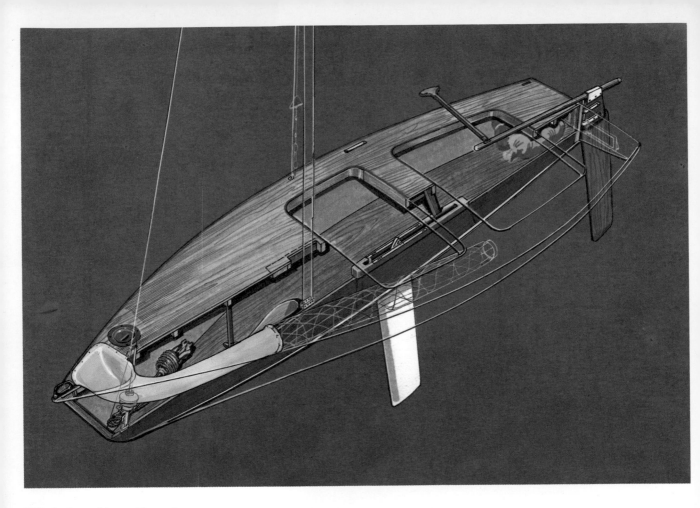

Weight distribution

For maximum performance the centre of gravity of a hull has to be as low as possible. This fact has to be borne in mind at a very early stage of construction. One might be offered a boat with a hull having a mahogany deck and a bottom made from a light type of wood such as gaboon or cedar, which would be no good at all. But the reverse, with a mahogany bottom and cedar decks, would be excellent since the centre of gravity would then be lower.

Of course it is best of all to build the whole boat as light as possible and then to bring the hull up to the minimum allowed weight by means of fittings of exaggerated weight placed low and amidships.

The weight of the hull has to be concentrated as much as possible towards the centre. In other words the bow and stern should be as light as possible and this has the effect of allowing the boat to move more easily in waves. So it follows that one must bear this fact in mind when fitting out the hull.

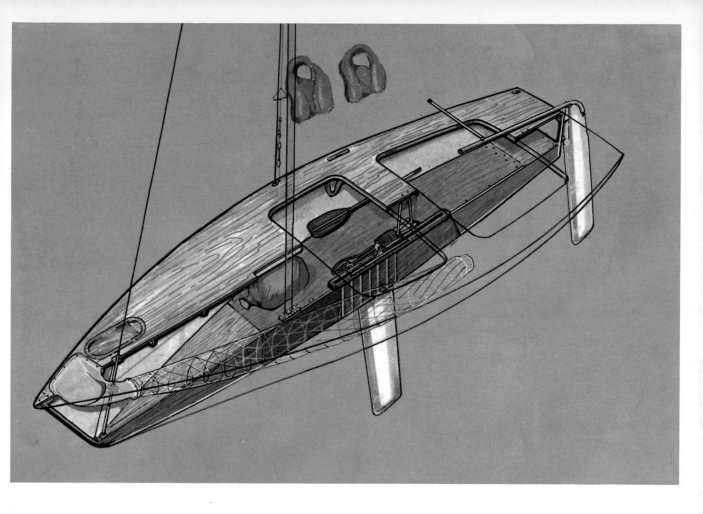

The drawings above show a typical (left) and a far better (right) weight distribution in a racing boat's hull and equipment.

Differences which can be seen include the use of lighter flooring under the fore and aft decks of the right-hand boat, lighter deck beams and coamings, the absence of a lifting handle and other weighty fittings at the stem, a lighter jib roller, a plastic sheet instead of an inspection hatch, a lightweight rudder, the paddle and anchor placed amidships, spare sails near the mast and not in the stern, life-jackets worn by the crew rather than being left under the aft-deck, plastic instead of heavy wood and metal transom flaps.

But even all these measures to improve the weight distribution of the hull can be nullified by the wrong positioning of the crew in the boat. The weight of the crew should normally also be concentrated, and therefore they must be sure to place themselves as close together as possible but their exact position fore and aft depends on the speed of the boat (see page 110).

Above: The crew, and also the spinnaker boom on the mast, are causing too much windage.

Below: The slot between mast and foresail is now completely unobstructed.

Above: Avoid unnecessary wind resistance.

Below: A clean outline from the use of skin-tight clothing.

Wind resistance

To achieve top speed to windward, wind resistance has to be reduced to a minimum. Often one thinks only of things like a smoother sailcloth but forgets the most important factors such as the windage of clothing, sail sheeting and spinnaker equipment and also rigging.

An important part of the total wind resistance can be eliminated by wearing tight clothing which also has the advantage that, when hiking out, it does not drag through the water. Trapeze systems which are adjustable for length, while being most effective, can nevertheless cause a great deal of turbulence between jib and mainsail. (See page 142)

When fitting out the hull, be very careful that as much equipment as possible is below deck level. If necessary, sink fittings into the deck.

The mainsheet system can often be improved by using thin ropes which reduce friction, and hence the number of blocks needed, and also by fitting wire strops between blocks and boom.

Above: Too much windage and weight.
Below: Minimum windage and low weight (See also page 90)

14

Of course other things like a flapping forestay, external spinnaker halyard and bulky spinnaker pole uphaul and downhaul are no good at all since they spoil the air-flow past the sails.

As can be seen from the deck plan of this top-class Flying Dutchman it is obvious that great trouble has been taken to reduce wind-resistance. There is no stem-head handle, the hatches are of plastic sheet, the spinnaker chute is sunk flush as are the compasses and the spinnaker and genoa fairleads are below decks. The traveller track would have been better mounted lower so that the lower sheet blocks would also be below deck level.

The rubbing strake is of minimum size except where the crew sit or stand so that they can hike outboard as far as possible. This feature also helps in concentrating the weights centrally.

Hull support on the trailer

It is probably true to say that a racing boat hull suffers more on a trailer than it ever does in a hard weather race. Most hull distortion is caused by bad trailer design and it should be remembered that the miles travelled when trailing are often more than those covered sailing. The trailer is not only a means of transport but it should also be a cradle to protect and support the hull.

Good suspension is of the highest importance and, since the all-up weight can vary, it is best to have torsional springing which is better able to deal with this.

To avoid shocks to the hull it should be tied down firmly using screwed rods or heavy straps. Concentrated points of loading should be avoided and rollers are examples of these. The best supports are those which are moulded to the hull shape and bear against bulkheads or beams. In any case the whole hull must be evenly supported. In general we can recommend supports about a quarter distance from the bow and stern (see drawings at upper right).

Two supports only are to be preferred since even the stiffest trailers bend in the fore and aft direction slightly. A trailer with three supports, when flexed, may support the boat only in the middle, or only at the ends, and the hull could be severely strained or damaged. The hull will certainly lose stiffness and strength and after a long trip it could sustain cracks. The left-hand illustrations make this clear.

Another cause of damage is the twisting of the trailer. In this case the forward support will be twisted out of line with the rear support and this is more likely to happen with the 'backbone' type of trailer where the main chassis is a single tube or girder (lower left).

If you want to keep your boat in top racing condition a first-class trailer is essential. One with an 'A-frame' chassis is likely to be stiffer in torsion (lower right).

Another thing one must take into account is the difficulty of getting parts for trailers and so spares should always be carried, including a spare wheel.

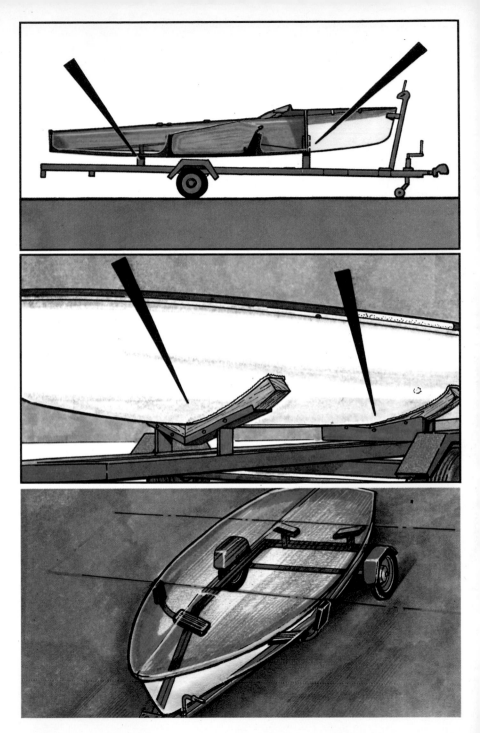

Chapter 2.
THE MAST

Materials

Ninety per cent of masts today are made from aluminium alloys. Wood has the disadvantage that it can warp with differing humidity and this also gives it variable bending characteristics so that it is impossible to standardize the tune of the rig. Fibreglass masts are not affected by humidity but they suffer the disadvantages of more frequent breakage and difficulty in attaching fittings.

The qualities of an aluminium mast depend on the particular alloy used and this has a tremendous affect on the 'spring' which is a vital characteristic. Too soft a material loses its spring due to metal fatigue which hardens the material.

Fatigue can be caused by the whipping of the mast when on a trailer and so, when trailing, the mast must be held as rigidly as possible. An easy way of stopping it from whipping is to secure it so that it is slightly bent.

Anodizing and welding also affect the bending characteristics and this fact should be borne in mind when comparing masts or testing unfinished sections.

Spreader fixings

Spreaders should be rigidly attached to the mast since, unless there is absolutely no play at this point the bending of the mast cannot be controlled via the spreaders. The leverage exerted by the spreader on its anchorage is very great and so this fitting has to be well designed and very strong. The spreader should be fitted so that it will bisect the angle that the stay makes in passing over its end. It is wrong to set it up perpendicular to the mast.

Spreader length and profile

The sideways bending of the mast is largely controlled by the spreader length though the crew weight and mast stiffness have an effect. Spreaders may be under compression, be neutral, or be in tension.

Spreaders under compression are longer than the distance from the stay to the mast and hence they push out the stay from its direct line. When sailing close-hauled only the windward stay is tight. The top part of the mast wants to bend to leeward under wind pressure but it cannot because the middle is unable to move up to weather, being resisted by the push of the spreader which is being held by the tight stay. The longer the spreader the greater the compression and hence the stiffer sideways is the mast. In light weather, because there is not enough wind pressure on the top of the mast, long spreaders can cause the middle of the mast to be pushed to leeward.

Neutral spreaders do not push or pull the stay out of line, but just touch it. As soon as the upper part of the mast tries to bend to leeward the spreader starts to push against the tight stay which limits the bend.

Spreaders in tension are shorter than the distance between the mast and the stay at that point. Hence, when close-hauled and the stay is tight, it pulls the mast to windward via the spreader and the top of the mast drops off to leeward.

The best shape for a spreader is a streamlined aerofoil section

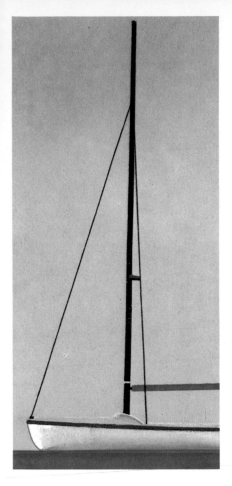
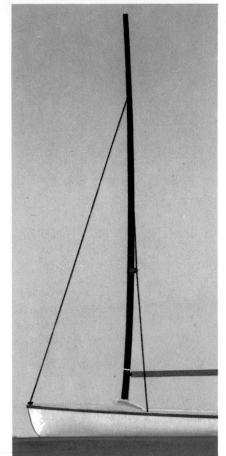
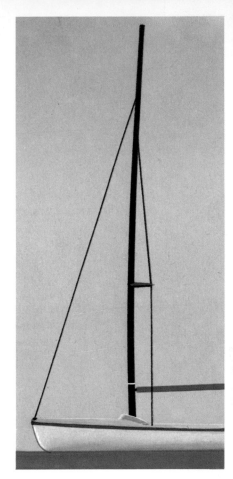

which is tapered. Round section spreaders bend too much.

Spreader angle

Spreaders which are fixed rigidly at the mast will limit the fore-and-aft bending of the mast. The windward stay, which is tight, supports the mast in the middle via the spreader, to which it is attached, and limits the amount the middle of

the mast can move forward. The top of the mast is therefore also limited in the amount it can bend aft.

If the spreaders are angled forward and fixed rigidly, the side stay will be pulled forward. When the windward stay is tight it therefore pulls on the middle of the mast and thus prevents the top from going aft. In light winds, spreaders fixed in this way can even pull the middle of the mast aft. One has to take care that the resulting bend is not too

extreme and in any case it should be taken out again with a moderate kicking strap or boom vang tension, which pulls on the masthead via the sail leach and pushes on the goose-neck via the boom.

Spreaders which are fixed in an aft-swept position can cause a big bend in the mast by pushing the middle forward when the stay is under tension. The more the spreader is angled aft the bigger the bend. This method is only used for very stiff masts. (See also page 70)

Mast support and control

To be able to control the sideways bend it is essential to hold the lower part rigidly. This can be done by fixing it at the heel and also at deck level in the mast-gate. There must be no sideways play whatsoever in the gate except in light weather when the mast can be allowed to bow to windward giving a little more width to the slot between mainsail and jib.

The best arrangements use the deck to support the mast. If there is no means of support at this point a rigid wooden or aluminium frame has to be made.

There are many types of mast control for use at deck level which are designed to enable the mast to take up a fore and aft bend and so adapt to various conditions.

In light airs the mast control will be rigidly fixed so that the lower part of the mast cannot bend. In more wind the control is adjusted to allow more bend. In the photograph this is accomplished by means of a nylon nut on a screwed rod. A control line is passed around the nut and led aft to the helmsman who is thus able to adjust its effect when sailing.

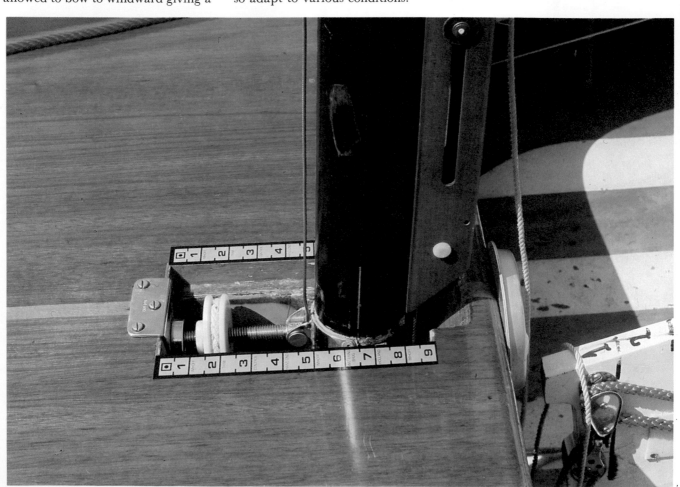

Control of side-bend

Side-bend has an immediate effect on the set of the sails and their interaction.

Firstly the slot between mainsail and jib gets wider. The effect is that the boat cannot be pointed so high but, on the other hand, it will be easier to hold it upright.

Secondly, owing to the top part of the mast dropping off to leeward, some wind pressure is lost by spillage off the freer mainsail leach.

There are also some other effects which are always adverse. Firstly the distance between the points of attachment of the forestay on the mast and at the deck will be shorter and therefore the foresail luff will sag. Secondly the mainsail shape deteriorates. In fact a sail-maker cannot make a satisfactory sail for a mast with a lot of side bend.

The good effects can however be achieved in another way without the disadvantages. For example a wider slot can be obtained either by raking the mast aft or by moving the foresail fairleads aft. It is also better to reduce sail power by letting the mast bend fore and aft so that the unsupported top then bends to leeward only in hard gusts.

How to increase side-bend

The sideways bending of the mast can be increased in the following ways:

1   Reduce the tensions in the side-stays (shrouds). For masts which are rigged with upper and lower shrouds each side, it is the upper shroud tension which should be eased in order to promote side-bend. Reducing the tension on diamond stays, for masts so rigged, will also have the same result.

2   Shorten the spreaders or move them lower down the mast.

3   Increase the side gap in the mast support at deck level.

4   Move the mainsheet traveller further to leeward.

5   Move the trapeze wire attachment point to a position below the shroud attachment on the mast.

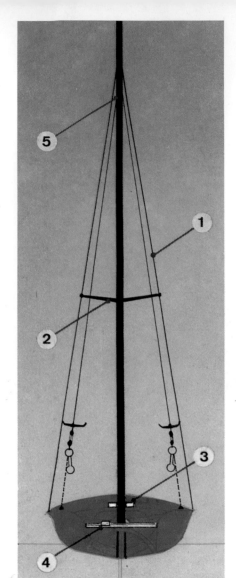

How to reduce side-bend

The same factors can be used to increase sideways stiffnesss but now they are applied in the reverse direction. They can be stated as follows:

1   Increase shroud tension. For masts rigged with upper and lower shrouds, it is mainly the upper which should be tightened. Diamond stays, where fitted, should be increased in tension.

2   Lengthen the spreaders or shift their position on the mast higher.

3   Fix the mast at deck level so that it has less side play.

4   Move the traveller nearer amidships, or even to windward of the centre line.

5   The trapeze wire attachment on the mast should coincide with that of the side-stay or be moved to a position above it.

Control of fore-and-aft bend

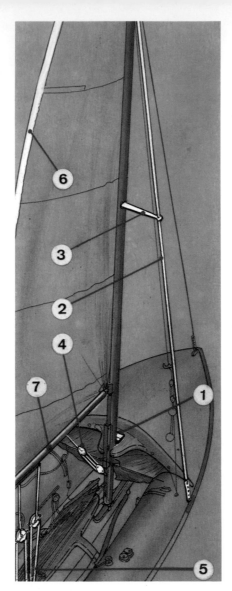

How to increase bending

The following methods can be used:

1 Reduce the thrust on the fore-side of the mast by the mast control at the deck. The effect will be to increase the bend mainly in the lower part of the mast.

2 Reduce tension in the side-stays (shrouds). If the boat is rigged with a back-stay to the masthead, the tension of this should be increased.

3 Swing the spreaders into a more swept-back position and refix them (see page 21).

4 Tighten the kicking strap (boom vang).

5 More tension on the mainsheet (but this should normally be done at the same time as the traveller is moved to leeward).

6 By changing to a mainsail with more round built into the luff and a tighter (more closed) leach.

7 Change to a stiffer boom.

How to reduce bending

The following methods can be used:

1 Increase the pressure of the mast control on the foreside of the mast at deck level.

2 Increase the tension of the shrouds. If there is a back-stay its tension should be eased.

3 Swing the spreaders forward and refix them (see page 21).

4 Reduce kicking strap tension.

5 Ease the mainsheet (usually in combination with the traveller being moved more to windward).

6 Change to a flatter sail with less round built into the luff and a freer (more open) leach.

7 Change to a less stiff (softer) boom.

Chapter 3.
THE SAILS

Headsails

It is of the utmost importance that the cloth at the luff of the sail is fixed to the luff-wire with the correct tension. If tension is too low horizontal folds will appear near the luff when the sail is set (see illustration at left). The set can be corrected by releasing the cloth from the wire and refastening it at a greater tension. Another possibility is to fit a cunningham hole near the bottom which has the added advantage that the tension can be changed whilst sailing. This is also of benefit when the sail is getting old and the material has stretched.

The opposite case, too much tension, is sometimes seen. The symptom is a deep fold close to the luff when the sail is empty of wind.

The luff tension also affects the camber of the sail. If it is slack, the point of maximum camber increases and moves towards the leach. If tension is high, the camber moves forward close to the luff and in consequence the leach becomes flatter. Therefore it is desirable to increase luff tension in hard winds and decrease it in light winds and hence a cunningham hole is usually the best answer.

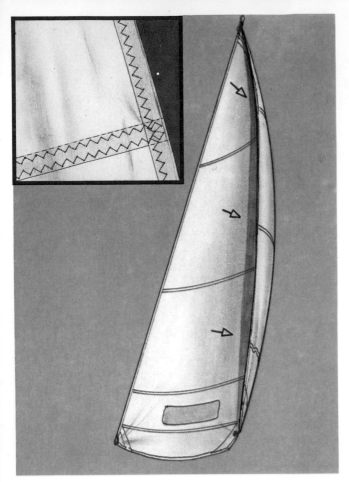

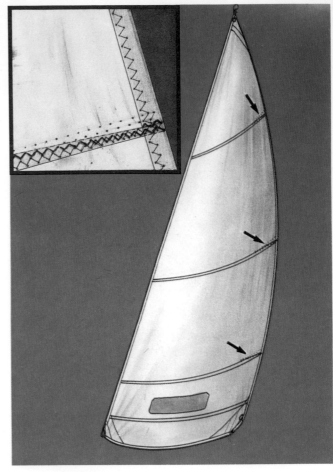

Correcting faults in headsails

Faults in the shape of a jib or a genoa can arise in two ways. Either it was incorrectly made in the first place or the fault has appeared after a period of sailing.

In the latter case, the material could be too light or of poor quality. Alternatively the sail may have been wrongly used. For example it may have been allowed to flog unneces-sarily in hard winds or it might have been set with too much leach tension.

If the fault is an original one it is usually easy to correct since the cloth will not have deteriorated with use.

The most common headsail fault is a tight, or curling, leach. The reason for this is that a single thickness of cloth will stretch more than the doubled and reinforced edge (tabling) and hence a sag can develop in front of the reinforce-ment which then hooks up into a curl. In genoas this is often prevented by cutting the leach edge with a hot knife instead of sewing on a rein-forced tabling.

Another way of opening, or loosening, the leach is to let out one more of the horizontal seams at the edge. It is the same as lengthening the leach by inserting narrow wedges of cloth. The above illustrations show the effect of this alteration and the details of how it is done. It is obvious that there is a limit to the

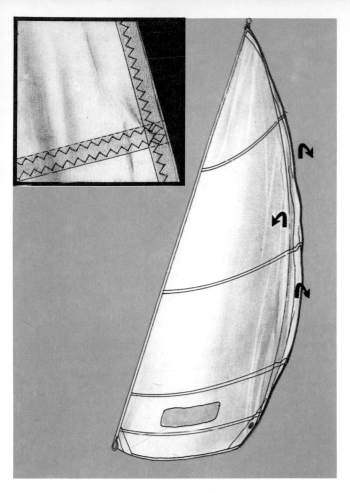

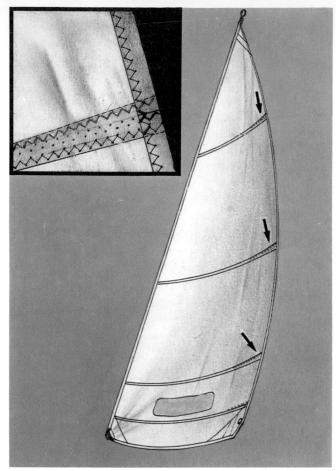

amount one can let out and still retain enough strength.

Another frequent, but not so serious, fault is a loose leach. This can vary from a vibration or flutter in the aftermost couple of inches, to a situation where the whole of the after part of the sail falls away.

In a hard weather headsail the former might be acceptable but in light winds it can be more serious. A very loose leach reduces the driving power of a sail and the boat is unable to point high. Furthermore, the fluttering of the leach causes turbulence which disturbs the all-important smooth air-flow between the jib and the mainsail, the area known as the 'slot' (curved arrows).

The method of correcting a loose leach is the opposite to the treatment for one that is too tight. In this case the edge seams have to be overlapped more which has the same effect as removing a narrow wedge of cloth. The illustrations make this clear. (See solid arrows.)

The amount of the adjustment is a matter of only a few millimetres. An experienced sailor can tell the amount and position of the adjustment needed. If he is unsure, then the problem should be discussed with a sailmaker, but the owner should give a careful and accurate description of the faults. It is no good just saying simply that the sail is not fast. Precise details of where faults lie, and how much adjustment is needed to effect a cure, should be noted down and passed to the sailmaker.

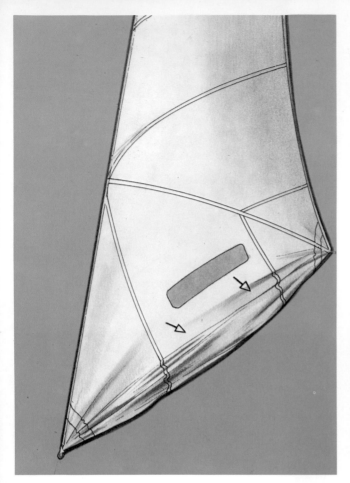 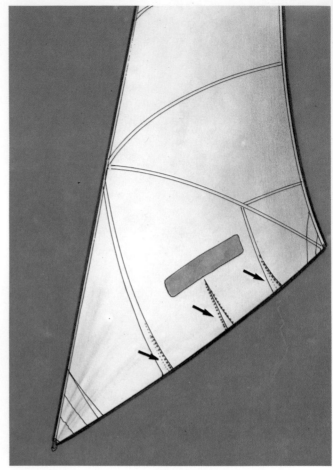

An often neglected part of the headsail is the foot. It is true that the foot has not the same importance as the luff or the leach but every small fault which can be corrected adds up to a great deal in total.

Improvement of a faulty foot (open arrows) is relatively simple since the amount of adjustment necessary is not nearly so critical as that required on the leach.

If the foot is too loose it can be corrected by taking up on the seams as shown in the illustrations above. Some extra dart seams can be introduced if required. If the cloths of the sail are all cut horizontally, darts are the only method of adjustment. (Solid arrows.)

The amount of adjustment depends on the amount the sail has stretched which can show as a slight flutter of the edge or can be a floging of the whole foot area of the sail.

The foot of a deck-sweeping genoa can be taken up so much that the edge cups inwards but this is no disadvantage—rather the reverse because it prevents air escaping underneath. With a high-cut foresail, similar to that in the drawing, the foot should lie nearly flat.

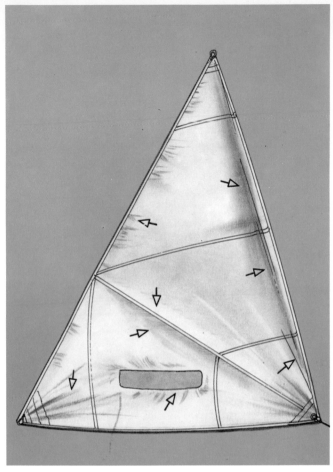

Faults that cannot be corrected

There are some faults which either cannot be corrected or can only be improved at great expense. It is then a question of deciding if it is worth the trouble or if a new sail would be the best answer.

The above drawings of two types of headsail give some examples of faults which are nearly impossible to cure. (Open arrows.)

On the left the sail has vertical cloths with seams parallel to the leach. If the leach is faulty, or the seams have tight ridges, it is nearly impossible to improve and obviously not by either of the methods previously described where adjustment was made to the seams.

On the right is a genoa where the cloth has become overstretched. This sail is completely worn out as is shown by the sagging hollow on either side of the mitre seam, the stretched and hooking leach, and also the puckers and folds at the tack and clew.

The life span of a sail before reaching this condition is not only measured by the amount it is used, but also depends a great deal on the weight and quality of the original cloth. It is false economy therefore to save money by buying sails made from cheap cloth.

Mainsail faults that can be improved

One of the most frequent mainsail faults, and one which eventually affects all mainsails, is a stretched and loose leach (see left). It is simple to correct by adjusting the leach seams in the same way as was done for the headsail (see page 29).

A tight leach, on the other hand, is not so easy to deal with owing to the reduction in seam overlap that is necessary. It is essential to have enough overlap to resist the very high loadings experienced on a mainsail leach.

Mainsail faults that cannot be improved

Unlike a headsail the shape of a mainsail is affected, and indeed to a great extent controlled, by the stiffness of the mast and boom and thus the outline shape of the sail has to match this bend.

The mainsail on the right has not enough luff curve to allow it to be set on such a flexible mast. This can be seen to be the case from the lines of stretch which go from the mast to the clew where the cloth has been pulled taut.

The sail cannot be altered. The only solution is a stiffer mast. The reverse, too much luff curve, is however easy to cure by removing a narrow strip of cloth.

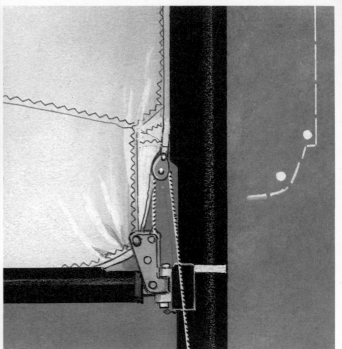

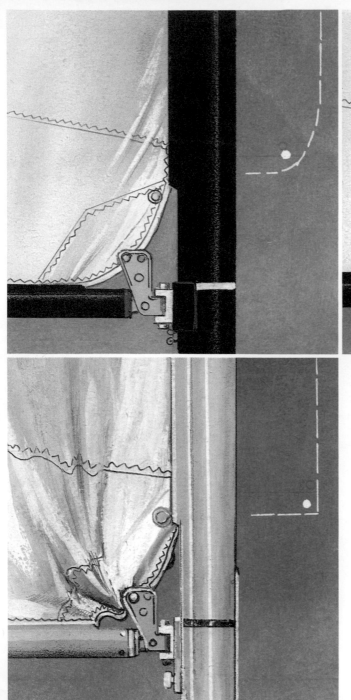

Another, but less serious, fault is a mis-match between the shape of the tack area and the position of the gooseneck pin. A poor fit here will put uneven strain on the cloth which can effect the whole shape of the sail.

Above can be seen two examples of a well cut tack whereas on the left it is obvious that the tack pin is wrongly placed being too low and not far enough forward.

Note the good arrangement for the cunningham tackle (upper, right).

Genoa faults—capable of improvement

Often a hollow appears on either side of the mitre seam especially near the clew. It is caused by the heavy loading transmitted via the sheet to this area of the sail.

The mitre seam consists of a double layer of cloth which thus has less stretch than the single thickness of the surrounding material which sags giving the appearance of the mitre being too tight.

This effect can usually be removed by releasing the mitre seam and re-sewing it with a little less overlap.

This operation is trickier if the two sides of the mitre seam are uneven; ie. one side may be cut straight and the other curved in order to create some special shape to the sail. In such a case it is necessary to unpick the whole seam including the clew reinforcing patches so that the inequalities in the lengths of each half of the seam can be worked out at the end. This is a much more complicated operation.

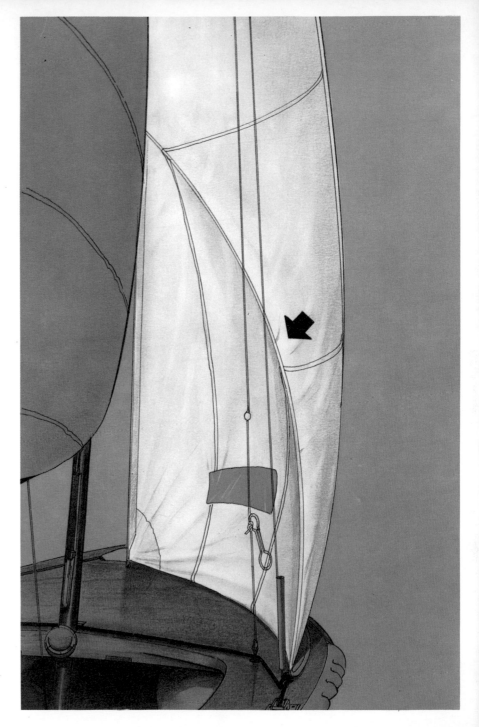

Genoa faults—not capable of improvement

An important genoa fault that is not repairable is one that inevitably occurs as the sail ages. The built-in camber gradually moves further aft and the outline of the sail also changes and this type of fault will appear quite quickly in genoas made from light material. They will thereafter only be of use in light airs.

The effect of sailing with such a genoa is that the boat does not accelerate in puffs and heels more than before. There will also be increased backwinding (luffing) of the mainsail. However a worn-out sail such as this can mislead the owner into thinking it is quite good since it will still enable the boat to point very high when close hauled owing to the flatter luff camber. The increased backwinding of the mainsail encourages the mainsheet to be pinned in hard and this also adds to the impression of pointing very high.

Moving the genoa fairlead aft does not help since, although the slot between mainsail and genoa is increased, the poor shape remains the same. The result will be worse pointing and no speed increase.

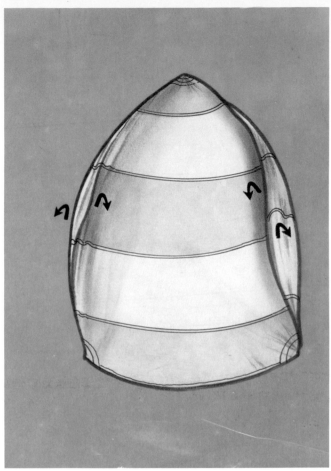

Improvements to spinnakers

Look hard at your spinnaker and carefully analyse its shape. It is a sail which needs more attention than is supposed on account of its very light cloth and relatively large area.

Also one can easily fail to realise the great changes in shape that occur over a season's use. It is similar to seeing a friend daily compared to

seeing him after a year's interval when all the small changes add up to a big difference. A good way of keeping track of these changes is to have the sails photographed at intervals.

The pictures above show faults in a new and unstretched spinnaker which can easily be corrected. The flapping areas are shown by the curved arrows.

On the left, the loose foot can be tightened as described on page 30.

The sail on the right has leaches which are too loose. This will correct itself with use since the cloth stretches more than the tabling. The process can be hastened by setting it often in hard winds.

38 This spinnaker is too flat at the top

.. and this one is too full

Spinnaker faults that cannot be improved

Spinnaker faults that cannot be improved include those caused by long use, as opposed to those discussed on the previous pages which were there in the sail when it was first made.

Inserting one or more new cloths into an old spinnaker is not likely to be satisfactory since the new material will gradually stretch whilst the old will have already distorted during its working life. Thus the initial improvement will lead to new faults as time passes.

The most common spinnaker fault is excessively hooked leaches shown in the photograph on the left. Such a sail has to be sheeted too close and hence gives too much backwind to the mainsail, while the greater side force will make it difficult to hold the boat upright.

There is not much that can be done to improve such a sail and it will only be effective in very light airs.

Finding hidden faults

We now know what the common faults are but can we just look at a sail as in the drawing and decide if it is, in fact, faulty?

Of course, some of these faults are obvious to everyone but many are not. To spot them one must get off the boat and look from the leeward side. It is essential for the helmsman to look at his boat with a very critical eye and from this outside viewpoint he will be able to get an entirely fresh look at his rig.

It is essential to get off the boat also to be able to check on the way the mast and sail are working together. Many factors affect a satisfactory match and experience plays an important part in deciding what needs to be done.

The reaction of the boat can give an indication of what is wrong. For example, if the mainsail is too tight on the leach the boat will carry a lot of weather helm and will not be easy to hold upright in the puffs.

On the other hand a mainsail which is too open on the leach will not point high enough and will be extremely easy to hold upright.

When close-reaching, some spinnakers collapse suddenly and without warning which can be most demoralising to the crew. The fault is either that the head area is too flat or that the leaches are too loose or too flat.

A mainsail which backwinds excessively at the luff in gusts and yet is very loose and open on the leach has been made with too much round on the luff and not enough shaping to the seams. This is an old-fashioned and unsatisfactory way of introducing the camber to the sail.

A genoa which is too tight on the leach can point high but acceleration will be poor and the backwinding of the mainsail will be excessive.

A genoa fault which is difficult to spot gives the boat the symptoms of a sail with a tight leach but nevertheless the sail looks a good shape.

The reason is a slight tightening of the leach seam right at the top. This small fault can have a very big effect on speed.

When to order new sails

There are two main occasions when an owner decides to order sails. One is when performance drops off to a noticeable amount. But by then he will already have suffered some poor results and will not be able to improve them for some time owing to the inevitable delay in taking delivery of new sails. Not only that, it will take some further time to trim the boat to obtain peak performance again.

Secondly, it is traditional to order new sails in the spring and this gives the sailmaker no chance to deliver them in time for the first races and it also cuts the tuning up period before the first races to nil. Often you hear after a race that has been lost, 'Well, it was the first time out with my new sails'. An inevitable result of ordering too late.

The right time to order sails is the autumn when the owner still has last season's performances in

'What do you think about a new genoa for next season, skipper?'

mind and can assess exactly what new sails are needed. Also the sailmaker is less pressed and can give the owner more time to attend to his special requirements.

Another point is that you will get in before the new-season price increases take effect or you might get a special winter discount. All this is in addition to getting the sails in plenty of time for early spring training and tuning which may show that some adjustments are required.

There is then still time to have them attended to.

Sail cloth

In USA—Dacron; in Britain—Terylene; in Japan—Tetoron; in France—Tergal; in Italy—Terital; in Holland—Terlenka; in Russia—

Lavsan; in Germany—Trevira. The chemical compositions of the yarns are all the same; the differences are in the way the cloth is woven and the after-treatment and finish that it is given.

The stability of the cloth depends on the tightness of the weave and the number of yarns to a unit area. In addition, the stability of the bias, or diagonally, is greatly improved by the finishing process which often takes the form of a coating of resin.

But this diagonal stability is obtained to some extent at the expense of stability in the length and width. It is necessary for the sailmaker to take all this into account when choosing the type of cloth he needs—stability primarily in the weft and warp, or primarily on the bias.

The first is preferable for mainsails owing to the heavy tensions put onto the leach (on the weft) and the second is best for a genoa where the main loading is in line with the sheet (on the bias). Therefore mainsail cloth should have less after-treatment than that used for a genoa.

The high-magnification photographs show, from top to bottom:

A loose weave sailcloth

A tightly woven cloth of about 190 g.s.m^2 (equivalent to $5\frac{1}{2}$ oz per English yd or 4.35 oz per US yd)

The same cloth after finishing by passing between hot rollers (known as heat-setting)

How to order new sails

How, first, do you pick the right sailmaker? You may be a person who gets to know one firm and always uses this same one. Or you might like to take advantage of the ease of ordering and getting your alterations done with the local sail-maker. Or perhaps another firm attracts you by advertising as being the cheapest. Or maybe yet another is well established at a local club and his sails score many wins (Top).

But for a sailor who wants top performance, these ideas, however attractive superficially, are quite wrong. You have to think inter-nationally.

Look around your class and find out what the champions are using. It could be safest to use the same. If you are already near the top and want to break through, it might be worth experimenting with some young and keen unknown, but this could be expensive.

Don't fall into the trap of getting all your sails from one maker. Look at the big winners and see that they often use different makes for main, jib and spinnaker and even others for heavy winds and light. There are specialists for every type and it is not necessary to have sails of the same make to ensure an aero-dynamic match.

When ordering your sails you can, if you like, tell the sailmaker such details as the mast and boom bend and the weight of the crew but it is seldom necessary to order anything other than a standard sail for light or heavy winds.

The sailmaker cannot, and will not, make sails to fit minute variations from boat to boat. Many owners try to persuade him to do this and that which will be certain to produce such a wonder sail that everything else is outclassed, without realising that the sailmaker would have done this already had he thought it possible. He, more than anyone, is keen to have his sails win, and will certainly advise his clients to have a basically standard sail to achieve this. Any variation is a risk which might rebound against him. If you insist on variations confine your demands to those you can back up with sound arguments and a knowledge of sailmaking practice.

The most important thing to tell the sailmaker is the conditions under which the sail will be mainly used. Heavy weather, light weather, general purpose, rough sea, ocean swells, smooth water, inland lakes.

Right
'The sailmaker cannot, and will not, make sails to fit minute variations . . .'

Below are shown examples of two very different genoas, both designed for medium wind speeds. That on the left is for use in rough water, whilst the other is for smooth conditions. The rough water sail is full at the bottom and rather flat higher up. The other is rather flatter overall and especially so on the foot. Apart from the design it is also worth discussing with the sailmaker the types of cloth he has to choose from. Tell him to recommend the best type and weight for the required conditions irrespective of price.

There are a few more points which should be clearly understood between you, such as the way you are going to set your foresail. Often nowadays, for example, one accepts a sail which is short on the luff measurement since this can have the big advantage of lowering the clew and closing the gap between foot and deck.

Another point is whether to have a heat-cut leach or a tabled edge. The sailmaker will advise when he knows the type of cloth to be used.

Sometimes somewhat shorter battens than the maximum allowed can improve the smooth overall shape of the sail and prevent the kink which is often seen at the forward end.

When choosing colour combinations for the spinnaker, think not only of an attractive and distinctive design, but more important—can the crew watch the sail intently without dazzle and can he see clearly the smallest lift or flutter.

Statistics show that the majority of sails that are bought are for light weather and this is astonishing. One suspects that they blow out of shape quickly and are then turned over to heavy weather use. This is utterly wrong since they cannot possibly have the essential forward camber and flat leach that only a sail intended for heavy winds and made from heavy duty cloth can have.

So, at the end of each season, list all your sails and assess carefully which need altering, which replacing and which can be kept for further good service.

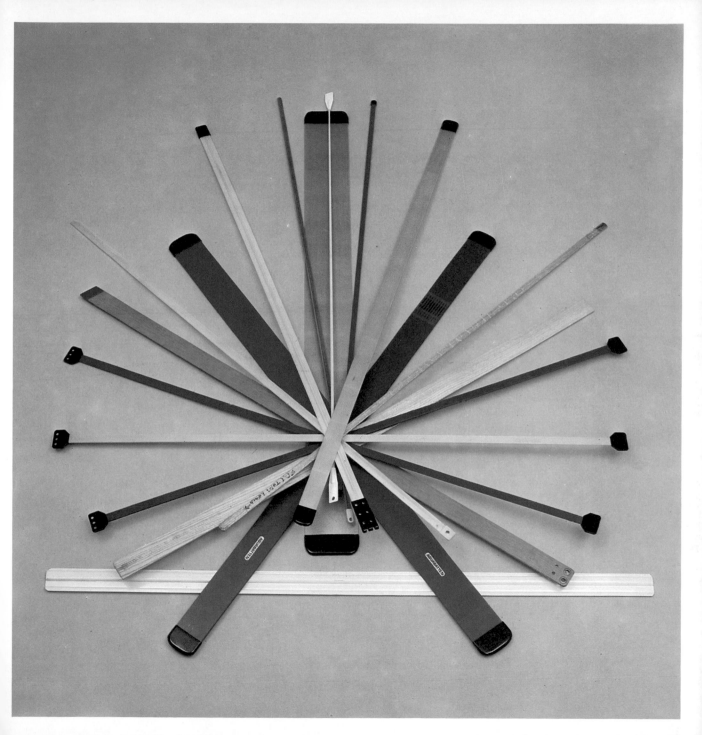

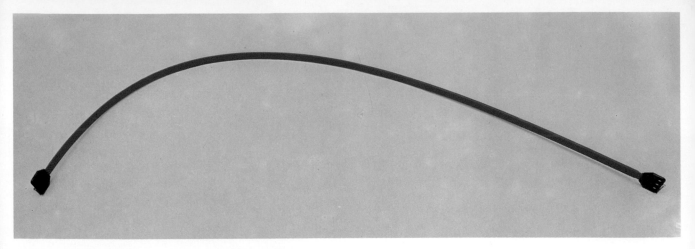

Sail battens

Each sail must have its own set of battens which are of a flexibility that is matched to the sail camber. Each batten must also go into its correct individual pocket and should be marked to this effect. (See photograph below) The arrow here indicates the forward end. 'L' is the mark for Light weather sail. 3 means that it is the 3rd batten from the top.

The ideal batten should be light, small in cross section, have graded flexibility getting stiffer towards the aft end (see above) and be generally more flexible for light weather sails to allow for more curve near the leach. Even heavy weather battens should still be flexible at the forward end to ensure a smooth transition to the unsupported cloth in front of them.

Modern unbreakable fibreglass battens are preferred to the wooden sort especially when they go the full width from leach to mast where the strains and possibilities of breaking will be much higher. The batten is held into the pocket under compression which is often adjustable by means of lacings to give more or less curve especially to the forward flexible end.

The flexibility of full-length battens can also be made adjustable by a wire from the head of the sail, passing over their outer ends and leading to a winch on the boom. Tension on the wire compresses the battens evenly and increases sail camber (see Page 60).

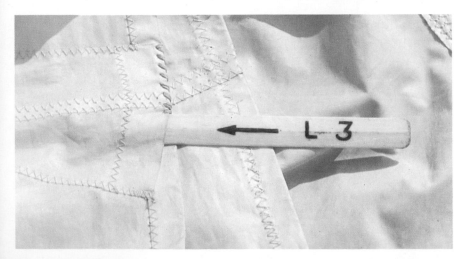

Telltales

Usually made from a length of wool or nylon, telltales are inserted about 20 cms behind the jib luff. They are used as a guide to accurate steering close-hauled, especially for genoas which are flat in the luff and which lift without warning, the weather side telltale flipping forward when the sail is set too close. If the lee side telltale becomes unattached and whisks about then you are sailing too free. Use a dark coloured wool so that its shadow can easily be seen through the cloth when it is lying against it. If both telltales are lying close along the sailcloth then the sail angle is just right.

Telltales can also be very useful on the mainsail in light weather to establish the best traveller position. The object is to ensure attached airflow on the lee side as far aft as possible. Wool tufts streaming aft indicate this (see drawing). If the tufts whisk about then that area of the sail is stalled and not producing maximum lift.

The principle for light winds is to bring the traveller to weather as far as possible without stalling the sail too much and by watching the shadows of several rows of tufts one gets a very impressive guide as to how far to go and how to vary the setting in different wind strengths.

Top: Sailing too free
Centre: Exactly right
Bottom: Sailing too close

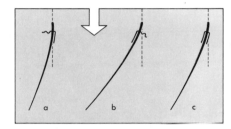

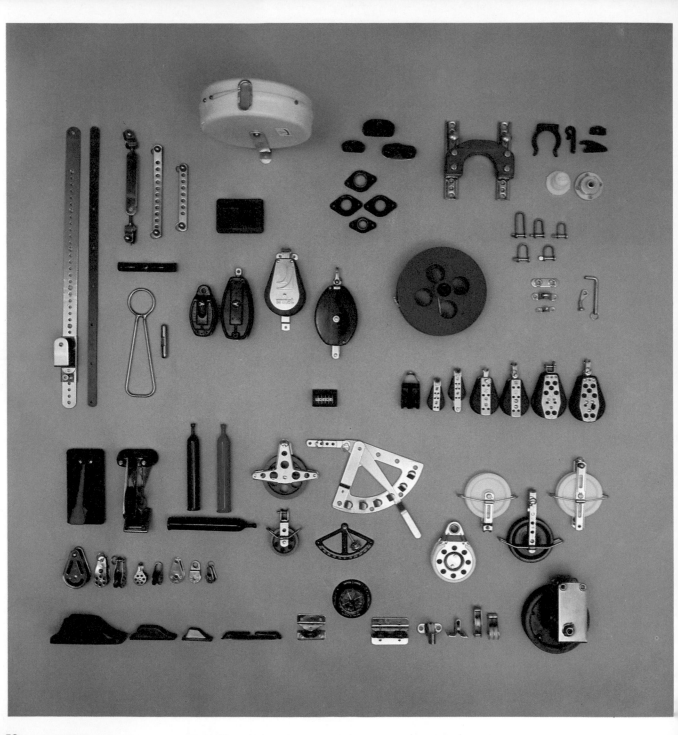

Chapter 4.
FITTINGS

The basic principle is that the equipment must work perfectly in all conditions and that the helmsman or crew must be able to operate it easily and without complication. So, for a start, a fitting must be placed so that it can be reached easily and does not get in the way of the crew's movements nor does it obstruct the working of any other piece of equipment.

Secondly the placing of a control line has to match the particular crew's routine and method of working, not forgetting such things as the way the crew hikes out and the positions where the helmsman and crew sit in order to trim the boat correctly.

Not only the positioning of the controls, but the whole layout of the cockpit should suit the way the crew works the boat, and this is greatly affected by the physique and height of each individual. This is why top-class boats are never absolutely identical.

Top: Control line cleats labelled to avoid confusion and angled so that they can be operated whilst hiking out.

Centre: A simple method of adjusting genoa halyard tension whilst hiking.

Bottom: A method of adjusting the jib fairlead on a 470 from the trapeze. Also, an automatic trapeze system (see page 142).

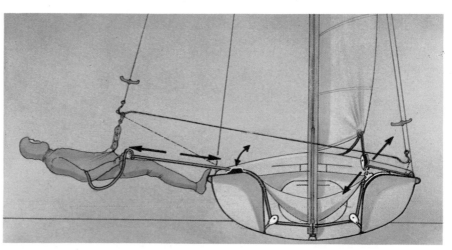

The correct placing of fittings

The top, left illustration clearly shows too great a concentration of controls which will make it difficult to adjust the lines without interference. An example of poor planning. Here, for example, the spinnaker and genoa sheets are so close together that the wrong one could easily be picked up. Another point is that the helmsman will certainly be sitting on the spinnaker guy when running and will be right on top of the cleats in light weather closehauled.

The top right photograph shows an underdeck spinnaker lead with the cleat mounted vertically on the coaming. A fairlead under the cleat ensures that the sheet is always in the right place. The deck is clean and unobstructed and the helmsman cannot sit on the sheet. Also seen is a tensioner consisting of a multiple sheave box.

Lower left is a frequently seen traveller arrangement which has disadvantages. The helmsman has to use his steering hand in order to adjust the traveller which is bad for concentration and accuracy of control. Also the angle of the cleat makes the direction of pull an unnatural one.

Lower right: the same traveller now has an improved system of controls. The free hand can operate the traveller easily and the direction of pull is arranged so that the line can be adjusted when the helmsman is hiking out and he can still concentrate entirely on steering without taking his eyes off the sails. The ends of the lines pass through the deck.

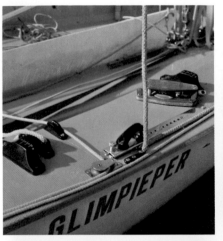

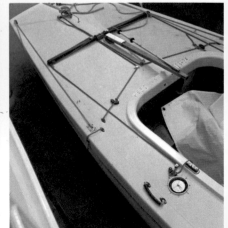

The illustrations on the right show a deck-mounted ratchet block fixed in three ways. The two methods shown on the left are wrong. The block should be placed so that the axis through the mounting points bisects the angle through which the sheet changes direction, as shown on the right. The side loading on the fastenings is then at a minimum.

Below is a spinnaker boom with a special quick action end fitting. The bail pivots on two pop-rivets and is connected to the plunger by a short wire. Either the bail or the line parallel to the boom is used to open the jaw thus saving a little time.

Another idea from this boom is the red fluorescent tape which enables it to be found immediately when it is under the deck in the shade even if the crew is dazzled by the glare off the water.

Other fittings which it is essential to position correctly are cleats and bailers. The cleats which hold control lines should be angled or chocked-up so that the pull of the crew on the rope, when in his normal position, is exactly in line with the cleat. Lead blocks should be fitted where necessary to achieve this.

Bilge water collects at the lowest point in the hull. When a racing dinghy is being sailed upright this is around the aft end of the centreboard case and so this is where the bailers

should be. In heavy winds the boat cannot be sailed so level and therefore a second pair of bailers further outboard might be worthwhile.

Remember also to protect the bailers from stamping feet. Siting them under a bridge deck or thwart might avoid possible damage in the rough and tumble of working the boat.

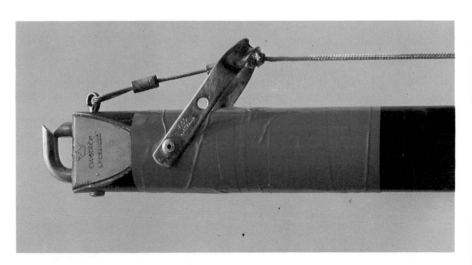

Great thought should be given to the positioning of fittings to avoid obstructing the crew in their movements. In particular, cleats, fairleads and winches should be so designed that, if they have to be on the deck and there is nowhere else they can go, they cannot catch in clothing or cut and bruise the crew.

The upper photo shows a poorly thought-out arrangement in which the crew will always be obstructed. The winch and the ratchet block are too close together and the lines can easily be confused in an emergency. The spinnaker sheet will be on top of the deck and will thus be sat on.

Below is a better arrangement, also on a Soling. The winch goes right forward, the spinnaker sheet and cleat are below deck, the traveller control cleat and mainsheet cleat are between the helmsman and middle crewman, and the compass is sunk flush. The helmsman's controls are near to hand and do not interfere with the crew.

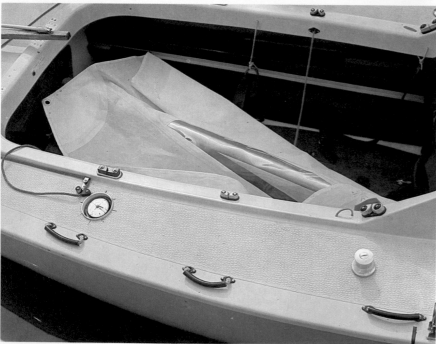

When mounting winches it is essential to remember that the axis of the barrel has to be perpendicular to the direction from the lead block. If it is not riding turns, which jam, will be sure to result.

Hardware is essential to the proper working of the boat and the siting of each piece is governed by its use. But the equipment and controls should be thought of as a whole because it is often necessary to make alterations to several items in rapid succession, as, for example, when rounding a windward mark :—

*Ease mainsheet
*Ease genoa sheet and re-cleat it.
*Raise centreboard.
*Hoist spinnaker halyard.
*Fix spinnaker pole to mast and sail.
*Cleat spinnaker guy.
*Adjust and cleat spinnaker uphaul and downhaul.
*Ease both cunningham tackles.
*Lower bailers.
*Tighten kicking strap.

In this type of sequence there must be no hold-up resulting from errors or jammed lines. The correct cleat or line must come to hand instantly.

Ashore when fitting out everything may seem to be fine, but under pressure in a race all sorts of things can go wrong. If, after a couple of races, it is found that all is not well be ruthless in thinking it all out again and in making the necessary changes. After all, what are a few holes when you are trying to win the next race!

On the boat in the lower, left photograph the cleat for the cunningham tackle is on side of the centreboard case. It seems a good idea because the line is short and simple and the cleat does not get in the way and is easy to fix.

However the cunningham hole is needed in freshening winds and the helmsman has to lean inboard to adjust it, losing righting power

and affecting steering at a vital moment (photograph, right). The few yards lost could be critical but could be avoided with cleats sited nearer to hand.

The right fitting in the right place

It is wrong to think that all your equipment can be bought from the same manufacturer's catalogue. You have to look very closely at each individual item that you need and obtain exactly the right one, modified as may be necessary, for each specific purpose. It may easily happen that three control lines will require three very different cleats, for example.

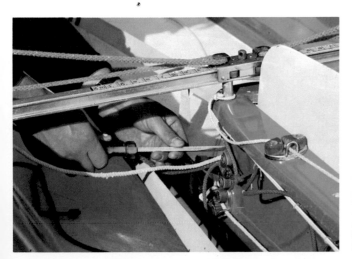

So consider particularly the following features:

Strength: Strong enough but not too strong! Too much strength means too much bulk and weight.

Weight: A little weight pared off each fitting can add up to a worthwhile saving overall, but never save weight if efficiency is thereby jeopardised.

Simplicity of action: All fittings must be absolutely foolproof to use and must work without fail in an emergency.

Design: Simple design means less can go wrong or break.

Look at each fitting with these things in mind and try to visualise how it will be used in practice on the boat. Take for example a simple D-shackle:

*What strain will it have to take (Strength)

*What should it be made of—stainless steel, brass, galvanised iron, aluminium alloy, nylon? (Weight)

*How is it opened? Pin with bayonet catch; screwed pin with eye; screwed pin with flat end; screwed pin with screwdriver slot? (Simplicity of action).

*Can it shake open? Has it got projections which could catch on something? Can it be opened easily? (Good design)

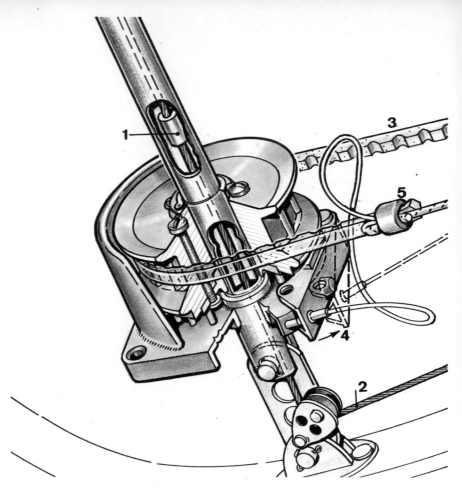

Some equipment is necessarily complicated—such as a jib-roller.

Firstly one should decide on the type of furling system that is needed which could be a simple nylon line wound round a drum or, at the other extreme, a ratchet operated drum-winch worked by pumping a lever or handle (see illustration).

The ratchet-roller was developed because of problems in operating the simple system which could easily jam up owing to the line rolling up incorrectly or becoming tangled. It was also slow and led to a great deal of loose line in the cockpit and two hands were needed to use it. On the other hand it was cheap and light and the line could sometimes double as the tail of the spinnaker halyard which saved a great deal of line.

The main advantages of the pump system are rapid one-handed operation, very fast unrolling with little chance of a foul-up, and also a cunningham control can be built in.

The cutaway drawing shows:

1   The cunningham wire with a swivel inserted, lying inside the revolving tube.
2   The cunningham wire led aft.
3   The toothed driving belt.
4   The pawl to prevent unwinding.
5   Shock-cord to return the toothed belt after each pull. Also connected to it is the wire to trip the pawl and so unfurl the jib.

Another excellent device is the multiple part tackle for tensioning the genoa halyard. It is a six or eight part purchase mounted in a box with one set of sheaves able to slide in the grooves. The genoa halyard is shackled onto the moving sheave-cage and the hauling part is led aft to a convenient position (see photograph, above right and page 22).

The tensioner can also be used on the shrouds, in which case it is mounted under the deck (see page 52). Other applications are for the backstay, the boom-vang, or the cunningham holes of larger boats. Modified to work a plunger it can be used as a mast-bend control at the deck.

A material which is as useful today as was shock-cord elastic when it appeared years ago, is velcro-strip. There are many places this can be used for fastening things temporarily. The photograph below, right shows a way of holding the spinnaker sheets ready for use using Velcro-strip on their ends and on the side of the splash rail.

The advantage can be clearly seen. The sheet comes away as soon

as it is pulled and there is nothing to snag and tear the sail as it goes up. Similarly the guy comes free at a tug and both can be re-fastened in an instant when re-stowing the sail. Another point is that weight is saved. There are many other opportunities to solve problems in such a simple and practical way.

Clear plastic sheet, obtainable at bookshops and elsewhere, can also be used with advantage. For example, the transom flaps can be replaced with this material stuck on, thus saving weight and making a watertight closure which is simply kicked out on capsizing. Plastic sheet can also be used for sealing inspection hatches and for covering sailing instructions and charts.

Making adjustments without tools is an important facility. Drop-nose pins instead of bolts and nuts; wire retaining rings for clevis pins instead of split pins are two examples of fasteners which need no tools.

Being able to switch over instantly from using a ratchet-block in

fresh winds to a free-running one when off the wind or in light airs is an advantage. Winch blocks with on/off switches are being built into swivelling mainsheet cleats and are well worth having.

Spinnaker sheets can be very troublesome in getting hooked over the outer end of the boom. A light line from a position 30 cm up the leach to the end of the boom can prevent this. You can also fix a small hook, opening aft, on the underside of the boom to keep the sheet out of the water in light airs and to hold it further outboard. Both these ideas are examples of things which are essential to a top-class boat.

Thought should be given to the best model of self-bailer, since there is a wide range of bailing capacity available and also there are some lightweight types made of nylon instead of stainless steel.

Bailers are usually carefully fitted into the hull but the way of operating them is rarely considered. Leaning inboard to open or close the bailer is a speed reducing factor. So why not work out a remote method of control?

The photograph, top, left, shows such an arrangement. The locking lever is removed and the bailer can then be pushed down with the foot whilst the helmsman is hiking out and closed tight again with the line led to a suitable cleat on the side-deck.

The centre photograph shows a simple design for a sliding gooseneck which has no clamping screw and needs no separate track. The extrusion fits the mast luff groove and can slide freely being fixed when needed by a pin at the lowest level allowed

by the rules. It has an integral tack fitting with several pin holes giving a wide range of positions to suit various sails. The whole design is functional, simple and saves appreciable cost.

Lower, right is a note-board made of white plastic and stuck to the sidedeck within reach of the helmsman. On it can be noted in waterproof wax pencil such valuable information as the compass headings between the marks of the course and the sail numbers of boats which

may be involved in protest incidents.

Other boards can be mounted to show flag signals, sailing instructions or courses for example. A very important use for a writing board is to note trimstrip numbers or suggestions for improvement and repairs to equipment or sails (see later).

Another fitting to include is a spinnaker sheet catcher, which is a short light wire projecting forward from the bow. It is only needed on classes of boats where the forestay is right on the stemhead and there is a danger of the sheet dropping over and going under the hull. On Flying Dutchmen and Solings, for example, this fitting is not required.

Self-tacking jibs were developed on the Star and are now seen on other boats which have high aspect ratio jibs, such as the Soling (see photo, right).

There is a single sheet, often of wire, which is led round a sheave in the bow and back to a traveller to which the clew of the jib is sheeted.

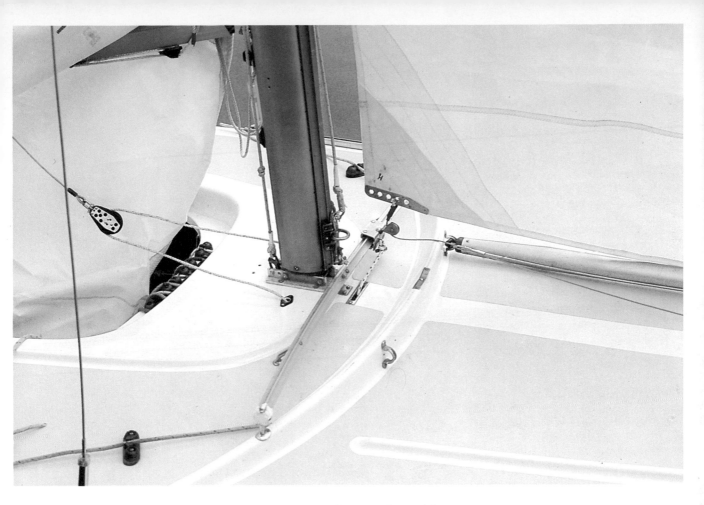

Thus the sheet is first set and cleated and then the jib can tack without further attention. The advantages are that the crew can hike fully until the last second and reposition themselves instantly on the other side, without touching the jib, and knowing that the setting on the new tack is exactly the same as the optimum setting found previously.

The athwartships position of the traveller is also precisely controlled by a wire and both wires can be adjusted by the crew from either side whilst hiking.

Fore and aft adjustment is available by means of a plate sewn to the clew into which the sheet is shackled (see photograph).

Slightly overlapping jibs can be dealt with by bowing the track forward round the mast but only a small amount of overlap can be accommodated.

As previously noted on page 48 the curvature of battens is of very great importance to the overall sail shape and particularly so in the case of full width battens. The photograph shows an excellent method of controlling the shape of a fully battened mainsail.

The wire through the batten ends is fixed at the top and leads to a purchase or a small winch at the bottom. Owing to the even convexity of the leach, extra tension on the wire compresses all the battens against the mast and gives them more curvature. Hence a greater camber is forced into the sail and so the same sail can be used in all winds and can also be varied for beating or running.

The winch can be sited on the fore end of the boom or on the mast so that it is within the crew's reach while sailing. Not many classes allow fully battened sails but for those that do, such as the Tornado Olympic catamaran class, the extra windage of the wire must be taken into account before deciding to fit the system.

A hook near to the gunwhale to lead the spinnaker guy at a lower level is essential on a trapeze boat since otherwise the guy would get in the way of the crew when he was using the trapeze.

The main problem in fitting such a hook is to prevent it snagging other lines such as the genoa sheet when tacking. Hence the folding hook shown above, right, is a very good answer.

The spinnaker pole end-fittings have to take very high loadings but must also be capable of being operated very fast. The left, centre photograph shows a simple hook with a rubber catch. It is fast but rather weak and also not absolutely secure. It can come unhooked at the mast in some circumstances or the guy can drop off.

Right, centre is shown a very strong end-fitting in which a spring loaded plunger closes the hook securely. It can be opened by the line or by pushing the 'V' notch against the eye-plate on the mast.

 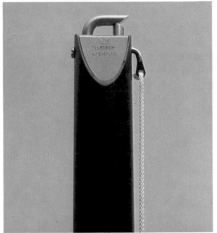

Sometimes it is not possible to fit levers or multiple purchases for the shrouds below decks. Below, right is shown a good type of turnbuckle with a built-in lever which, when closed, also locks the screw by pressing against the side of the nuts.

This is another example of a fitting which can be adjusted without tools. Notice also the good universal joint to the chain plate at the bottom.

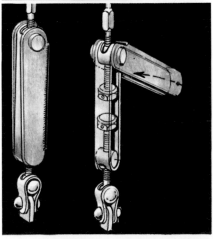

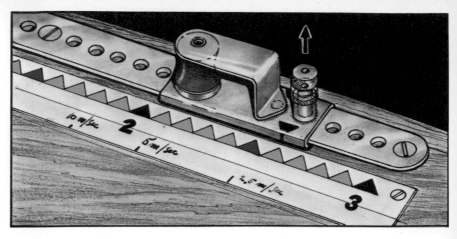

Accurate control of adjustments

It is essential to make all sorts of adjustments to the boat to obtain top performance in varying conditions of wind and sea. You must first take note of the correct positions for all the variables on your boat in certain standard sets of conditions and it is then easy to be sure that this trim is repeated whenever those conditions arise again. You can find certain key trim positions for fittings by looking at the top boats in your class and then marking your own boat clearly.

Some examples of good positive adjustment systems are shown. Above is a sliding fairlead with a spring-loaded plunger which enters one of a series of holes in a track. This has a big advantage over a fixed fairlead since, by numbering or marking the holes, the best position can always be repeated.

Below is a method of making fixed adjustments to a control line or wire where the swaged-on balls drop into a keyhole slot. This is better than a cleat and it makes the crew's work much simpler when the helmsman can say to the crew 'Set

the shrouds at number three and tighten the genoa halyard two positions'. There is then no room for doubt.

It is even better to number the positions for the corresponding wind force or wind speed. Then your crew knows for sure that if the wind is force three, all the adjustments should also be at position three. (See illustrations).

It is not always possible to do this as each sail is different and needs individual adjustment but the use of

scales and marked points avoids the vague type of order 'Tighten a little on the genoa halyard'. And then a conversation can start 'Is that OK' 'No, too much. Let it out a bit.' and so on. The result is irritation, loss of concentration and reduced speed whilst the right trim is being re-established.

Some examples of the application of this principle are shown on the right. Note the boom-end, the traveller and the jib fairlead. Other useful applications are on the centreboard where its position can be

Trimstrips

It is not possible to arrange for all adjustments to be made in fixed steps by means of pins and holes or with swaged balls and keyhole plates. For these you should use some marking system such as painted symbols on the deck, but it is easiest to stick on trimstrips which can now be bought in many boat shops.

These trimstrips, which are lengths of self adhesive plastic with clearly marked numbered scales, can be put alongside any movable fittings such as, on the boom by the clew outhaul, on the deck by a fair-lead, on the traveller track, on the mast by the cunningham hole, on the foredeck by the mast control (see page 22), or on the floor by the mast heel for example.

located positively with a spring-loaded plunger which can enter one of a row of holes: again, a lifting rudder blade can be adjusted more accurately by the ball and keyhole system rather than a plain line and cleat. Similarly the spinnaker pole uphaul and downhaul should be a wire with swaged-on balls. Again, strip-metal adjusters with pins and holes can replace rigging screws. Marks on the gunwhales show where the trapeze man stands in various wind strengths and also notches can be cut to locate his feet. A kicking strap wire with ball and keyhole adjustment ensures that fixed tensions can be repeated.

Using trimstrips with logsheets

It is impossible to remember all the combinations of adjustments necessary for all wind-speeds, sea conditions and different sails. So log sheets should be used to note the best trim in each situation, using a different sheet for every combination. Both good and bad results should be noted on the logsheets.

Tuning the boat is then a logical result of analysing data from the logsheets and the results can later be transferred to the trimstrips or other marking system. The more data that is available, the less chance there is of error.

On a good logsheet all the factors which might have a bearing on the best trim will be mentioned so that, after a race, it is only necessary to fill in the trimstrip numbers and the weather and sail details.

It is obvious that different classes of boat will need different entries on the logsheets. Owners can either make their own logsheets or they can use standard forms which are available and are designed to cover most types of boats.

If this system is to be of benefit, the logsheets must be conscientiously filled in after each race, not only entering good trim and successful results but also including failures and the reasons for them. There will then be little danger of setting the boat up with a poor trim in a misguided effort to find something new and faster because it will already have been noted as being an unhelpful combination.

Don't forget to note such things as wind strength, sea and wave conditions, weight of crew and whether wet clothing is worn and, of course, details of the opposition.

We have already seen that certain sails are designed to perform best in, say, choppy waves and others in flat water. Similarly the trim will vary in different conditions. After a season's sailing it should be possible to know very closely the correct trim of the boat for a number of sets of conditions, by sorting out the mass of detail from the filled-in logsheets. Sometimes some surprising results show up and point the way towards a successful campaign next season.

After a firm conclusion has been made concerning one set of conditions a master logsheet should be filled out and this master should be taken to every race meeting and will form the basis for setting up the boat on arrival.

Master logsheets should also be kept on board larger keel-boats so that the trim can be checked and adjusted against the relevant master during sailing. This is not possible in centreboard boats or light keel-boats. Here, therefore, is another use for your note-board since the basic information for increase or decrease in wind can be marked up in wax pencil on this board.

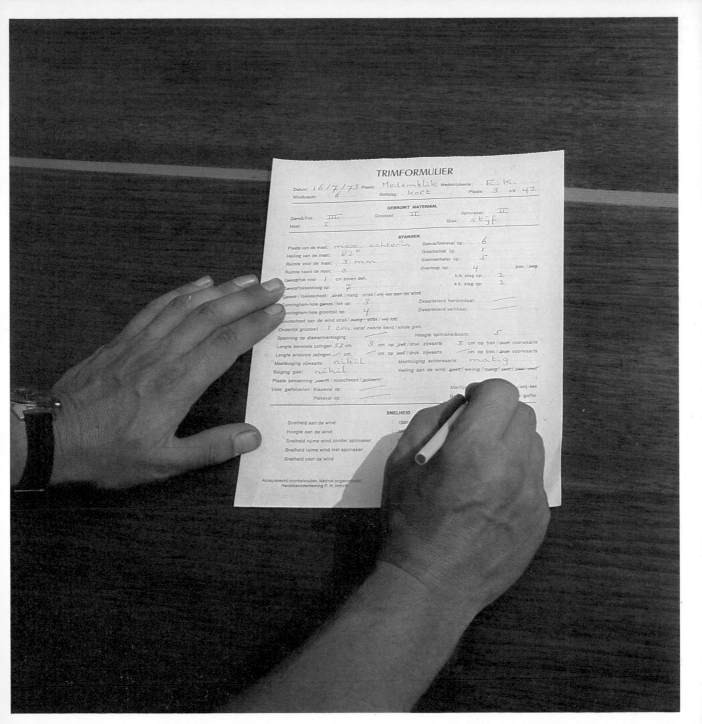

TRIMFORMULIER

Datum: 16/7/73 Plaats: Medemblik Wedstrijdserie: E.K.
Windkracht: 6 Golfslag: kort Plaats: 3 v/d 42

GEBRUIKT MATERIAAL

Genua/Fok: III Grootzeil: II Spinnaker: II
Mast: I Giek: stijf

STANDEN

Plaats van de mast: max. achterin	Genua/fokkeval op: 6
Helling van de mast: 82°	Grootzeilval op: 1
Ruimte voor de mast: 3 mm	Giekneerhaler op: 5
Ruimte naast de mast: 0	Overloop op: 4 .... pos./neg.
Genua/fok voor 1 cm boven dek.	
Genua/fokkeleloog op: 7	b.b. stag op: 2
Genua/fokkeschoot: strak / matig / strak /vrij-los aan de wind	s.b. stag op: 2
Cunningham-hole genua/fok op: 3	Zwaardstand horizontaal:
Cunningham-hole grootzeil op: 4	Zwaardstand vertikaal:
Grootschoot aan de wind strak /matig / strak / vrij los.	
Onderlijk grootzeil 1 cm vanaf zwarte band / einde giek.	
Spanning op diamantverstaging:	Hoogte spinnakerboom: 5
Lengte bovenste zalingen 53 cm. 8 cm op trek / druk zijwaarts 3 cm op trek/druk voorwaarts
Lengte onderste zalingen ... cm. ... cm op trek/druk zijwaarts ... cm op trek / druk voorwaarts
Mastbuiging zijwaarts: nihil	Mastbuiging achterwaarts: matig
Buiging giek: nihil	Helling aan de wind: geen / weinig / matig / veel / zeer veel
Plaats bemanning: voorin / midscheeps / achterin:	
Voor gaffelzeilen: Klauwval op:	Marlijn .... / vrij-los
Piekeval op:	B ..... gaffel

SNELHEID

Snelheid aan de wind	zeer
Hoogte aan de wind	zee
Snelheid ruime wind zonder spinnaker	
Snelheid ruime wind met spinnaker	
Snelheid voor de wind	

Auteursrecht voorbehouden. Nadruk ongeoorloofd.
Handelsonderneming F. H. Imhoff

Part Two—BOAT TUNING

Chapter 5.
SETTING UP
THE BOAT

Mast position and rake

When setting up the rig on the boat ashore the first thing to decide is the position of the mast. A simple guide cannot be given because the ideal position varies from boat to boat.

A newcomer to a class must pick the brains of the old hands to get a basis for starting tuning his own boat. There are, of course, basic rules such as—too much weather helm needs the mast to be moved forward, and vice versa. In a centre-board boat excess lee or weather helm can also be cured by adjustment to the centreboard (see page 92).

But there are exceptions. In boats with large overlapping genoas, weather helm can occasionally be reduced more effectively by moving the mast *aft* because then the slot between mainsail and genoa becomes wider. In a boat with a normal jib of very little overlap this effect depends on the position of the jib fairlead athwartships. If the fairlead is moved more inboard, weather helm may increase, and the mast may have to be moved further aft and vice versa.

Above
Normally the mast should be raked forward for running.

Left
Normally the mast should be raked aft for beating.

In considering mast rake there is a general rule that for close-hauled trim it is better for the mast to rake aft (see photograph on left). An exception is in light airs when an upright, or even a forward raked mast, can prove best.

An important point to remember is that moving or raking the mast when close-hauled alters the shape and width of the slot. If the fairleads are left in the same place, raking the mast also alters the tension on the headsail leach.

This effect can be used very simply to alter the tuning for an increase in wind strength by raking the mast more aft. A wider slot and looser jib leach results which is exactly what is needed. As discussed on page 98 the boat will go faster but will point a little lower and will be easier to handle.

For downwind sailing, forward rake is always best and the mast heel should come aft too if possible. One reason this works is that it allows the main boom to be eased out more, (see photograph on right). But there are other more complicated aerodynamic benefits too.

Do not make the mistake of assuming that aft mast rake and aft mast bend are the same thing. The reasons for their use and the resulting effects are quite separate.

The helmsman has to assess the different problems and make adjustments either to the rake or the bend or a combination of both in order to arrive at the best result. The only way to make a proper assessment is by noting on the log-sheet the trim-strip numbers and the effects of individual adjustments. The matter is further complicated by side-bend but the analysis is made quite straightforward by referring to the log-sheet.

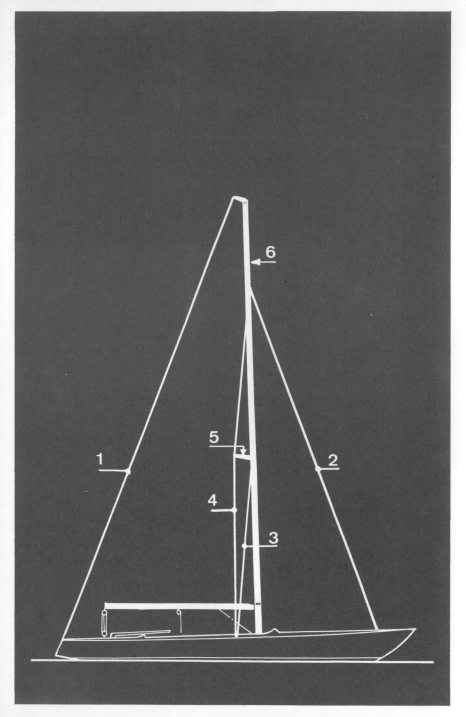

Shroud and stay tension

A great deal of thought should be given to the various pieces of standing rigging, their relative tensions and the effects they have on each other, the spars and eventually on the all important sails. The diagram shows the rigging of a typical 'Soling' which demonstrates about the most elaborate rig likely to be found on a small boat and hence is a useful model to discuss.

When setting up any mast it is essential to start by getting it perpendicular to the deck on a hull which has been levelled up. Then mark the rigging adjusters to give a basic reference point. Use only enough shroud and stay tensions to hold the mast straight and steady. Now, further tension can be applied to the turnbuckles equally as needed.

The use of a backstay (1) is twofold. Tighten it and you also tighten the forestay (2) which is essential for close-hauled performance. Secondly the mast can be pre-bent by pulling the top part (6) aft. The amount of bend and its relationship to forestay tension can be controlled or limited by varying the tension on the lower shrouds (3). At times these may be quite slack and many rigs have the lower ends fixed to a sliding track on the deck, or have some other means of making rapid adjustments for differing conditions.

Easing off the backstay when the wind is aft, not only lets the mast rake forward as is normally required, but it also slackens the forestay giving more fullness to the jib, while at the same time the lower shrouds hold the centre of the mast stiffer, thus putting more camber into the mainsail.

Turning to side-bend, the effects of having more or less upper shroud tension and the effects of longer or shorter or more angled spreaders have been discussed on pages 20 to 25. The extra pair of shrouds shown here give added possibilities for adjustment.

Normally, if the mast is to remain without side-bend when close-hauled, the upper shrouds (4) will need to have more tension than the lowers (3) owing to their greater length and loading and hence greater stretch. Less upper shroud tension means that the upper part of the mast can bend off to leeward more.

Further possibilities are given by moving the lower anchorage of either or both pairs of shrouds more forward or more aft, and by clamping the spreaders rigid or allowing them to swing fore and aft a predetermined amount. In general moving the shrouds forward gives more side control to the mast and less fore and aft control and vice versa.

Many people guess the tensions in the rigging but it is better to use a tension gauge (see photograph). Finally re-check that the mast is not leaning off centre by dropping a weighted line from the masthead.

Below
Using a shroud tension gauge.

Luff tension in head-sails

In discussing luff tension in headsails it must first be clearly understood that there are, not one but, two separate tensions to be considered.

A headsail has a built-in luff wire which is set up with a certain tension. But there is also the tension of the cloth of the luff relative to this wire which is either set by the sail-maker at his loft or can be arranged to be controlled by a cunningham hole or adjustable tackle.

Halyard tension, which is transmitted to the luff wire, has to be high enough to prevent appreciable sagging of the luff away from the ideal straight line. Halyards must therefore be of wire and not rope which has too much stretch. A sagging luff is a direct cause of poor pointing ability (see drawing, left).

A sagging luff also throws more camber into the sail and causes the leach to close so that the boat is hard to hold upright (see drawing, right).

Boats can either be rigged with the foresail luff hanked to the forestay or left flying free. In the latter case it is essential that the luff wire takes all the load when the foresail is set and the forestay then only acts as a preventer for emergencies and for when the sail is lowered. Not as is happening in the drawing on the right.

The cloth tension along the luff controls to a large extent the position and the amount of the camber in the sail. Greater tension pulls the camber forward, flattens and opens the leach —an advantage in strong winds. Less tension increases the camber and moves it more aft giving the more even entry and tighter leach which is necessary for light airs.

Thus the control of the cloth tension is vital to top performance and this can easily be arranged by fixing the luff of the sail only at the head. A cunningham cringle is then sewn into the reinforced tabling near the tack and connected to an adjustment system conveniently placed for the crew. (See also page 27 et seq.)

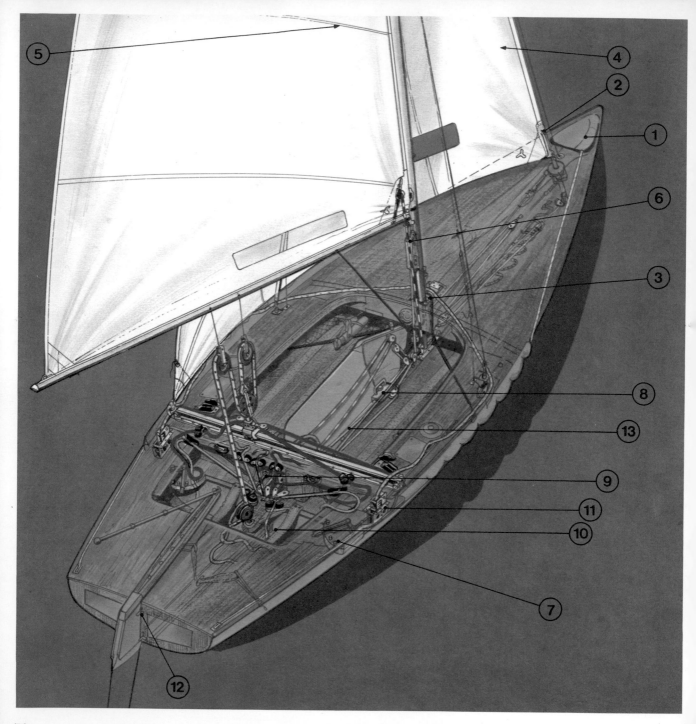

Final checks ashore

Before going afloat each time you should always check that all is in order with every detail of the boat. So make a check list suitable for your own particular class and go through it carefully. Here is an example of such a list:

Check the following items:

1 The spinnaker is rigged ready for hoisting.
2 Foresail luff tension (final adjustment afloat by cunningham hole).
3 Position of mast control at deck.
4 That there is no free movement in spreader anchorages.
5 That the correct battens are fitted.
6 Foresail halyard tension.
7 That standing rigging tensions are suitable for today's conditions.
8 Centreboard pivot position.
9 That all control lines are free and clear to work.
10 That bailers are working correctly and are closed for launching.
11 Fairlead positions are correct for today's conditions.
12 That the rudder and its fittings have no free play.
13 That the bottom and centreboard slot are clear of dirt or debris.
14 That all the equipment required by the rules is on board.
15 That the sailing instructions, course card and protest flag are on board.

Such a simple list can avoid troubles and breakages if checked out automatically before each launching.

Chapter 6.
COMPASSES

The basic features

Many helmsmen still only use compasses on open water when there is no background to guide them visually into finding the next mark. Many others fit compasses because it makes the boat look professional, but they don't know how to use them.

Compasses, used correctly, can make a big contribution to better racing results and can eliminate a lot of, so called, bad luck. The choice of the right compass is important and the desirable features include:

*Able to be read easily under all circumstances, even when hiking out.
*Not easily damaged.
*Has a card with minimum oscillation.
*Able to be mounted where it does not obstruct.
*Light in weight.
*Sufficiently gimballed to suit the amount of heeling expected.

It is often better to have a pair of compasses mounted in the side decks close to the helmsman rather than one mounted centrally.

76

Detecting wind-shifts

The wind normally shifts rhythmically about a mean direction and to discover the timing of this rhythm and the extent of the shifts you have to spend some time sailing to windward before the start watching the compass carefully.

For example, on port tack the boat's heading may vary from 100° to 120° and on starboard tack from 10° to 30°. With this information on the note-board it is easy to see at any time during the race what the wind is doing relative to the mean and hence, which is the favourable tack.

However, the wind does not always shift like this. The illustration shows three boats on port tack. Assume we are in the middle boat close-hauled and aiming exactly at a fixed point ashore. On closing the shore we are still exactly laying the fixed point—thus the helmsman thinks that he must have sailed in exactly a straight line in an unchanging wind.

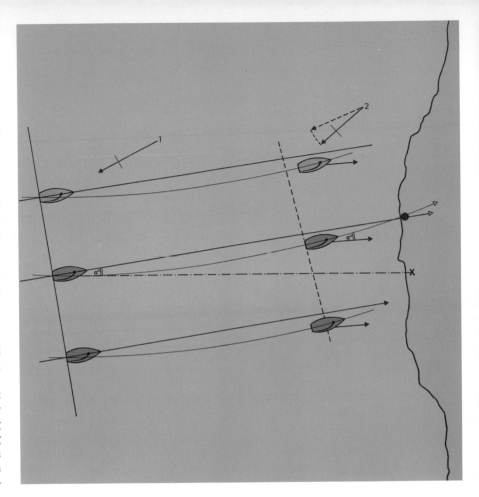

However, this cannot have been the case since all boats sail with a certain amount of leeway (angle α) and we ought to have arrived some distance to leeward of the fixed point ashore and would in fact have followed the dotted line to point 'X'.

Assuming there was no current, the explanation must be that the wind has slowly and steadily backed (shifted counter-clockwise) and the boats have made good the course shown by the curved tracks.

The effect on the relative positions of the three boats is that the windward boat gains most and the leeward boat least. The windward boat is relatively further ahead and appears to the others to be sailing faster, which is in fact quite wrong.

Had we watched our compass we should have spotted this very slow wind-shift and then the correct move would have been to tack to try to retrieve the loss. By carrying on we can only lose more.

This sort of incident, if it is not immediately recognised for what is, can be utterly demoralising to a crew who are misled into thinking their boat is slow and will then perhaps make unnecessary, or even retrograde, alterations to their trim.

So treat a bearing on a fixed point with reserve, since it is easy to forget about leeway.

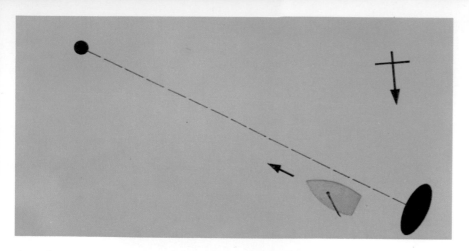

On courses where the relative positions of the marks are known, such as the standard Olympic triangle, the headings between buoys can be noted.

For example, point the boat at the first mark and note the course, deduct 135° (if marks are to be left to port) to obtain the course on the second leg, and deduct another 90° for the third leg. The run is the reciprocal of the windward leg course.

The compass can also be used as an aid to tuning to obtain the best pointing angle with respect to the apparent wind while using different combinations of sails and sheeting. Keel-boats can fit special multiplying compasses which gives this angle very accurately on an expanded scale.

At the start

If the start is to windward it is easy with a compass to find the most favourable end to start.

First point the boat directly into the wind, read the boat's heading and mark it on your note-board. Then immediately, and before the wind has a chance to shift, sail exactly along the starting line. Mark the course down.

If the difference between these two headings is less than 90° you are sailing towards the more favourable (ie windward) end, and your start should be made near the port end buoy (see upper drawing).

On the other hand, in the lower drawing, the difference between the courses would have been over 90° and therefore you would be sailing away from the best end.

Check the angle several times to eliminate errors caused by wind-shifts.

At the lee mark and the windward leg

If the leading boat around the lee mark has no compass she will be lucky if she starts the windward leg on the most favourable tack.

The second boat will almost certainly take the opposite tack initially and, if the leader is on the wrong one, the second boat must certainly gain. So the leader must work out in advance whether to sheet in round the mark and continue on the same tack or whether to tack immediately at the buoy.

The technique is to note the extent of the wind-shifts on the note-board before the start and

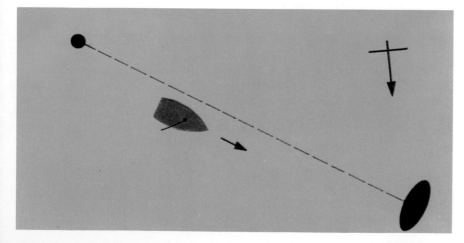

again on the first beat. Then, as soon as you come hard on the wind after rounding the mark it can immediately be seen from the compass heading whether you are sailing on a favourable tack or not.

The second boat will then either have to tack onto the unfavourable tack or must remain in the windshadow of the leader. The upper drawing shows a typical situation in three stages.

Brown tacks at the buoy and the blue boat, which is just leading, continues and then tacks to pick up the backing wind-shift which is a heading shift for brown, and makes another gain. Finally she tacks to cover the brown boat from a commanding position.

If the brown boat had a compass she could have limited her loss at the beginning by continuing behind blue immediately after the mark, knowing that this was the favourable tack to be on.

In the illustration the brown boat tacks for the second time exactly when a backing wind-shift arrives, which is exactly the wrong moment. Again, if she had a compass, she would have been able to detect the backing wind-shift and would not have tacked until it had veered again.

Use the compass to tell whether you are ahead or astern of another boat by sighting at about $45°$ to your own heading. You can also judge when you can tack to lay a mark by sighting approximately abeam, the exact angles being found by experiment.

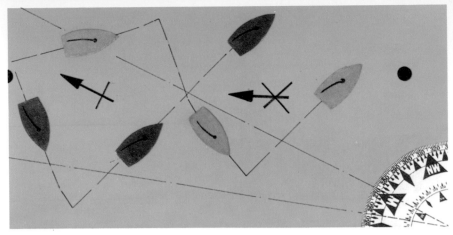

At the windward mark

You should also use the compass to determine the gybe for the downwind leg and you can do this before you reach the windward mark.

In the case shown in the lower drawing the blue boat saw on the compass, just before reaching the buoy, that the wind had veered and so she set off downwind on the port gybe and was ready to go onto starboard gybe when the expected rhythmic backing shift appeared halfway down to the lee mark.

Brown, on the other hand, has no compass and set off on a starboard gybe, changing to port when the wind-shift arrived. Not only has she sailed a longer course but she is on a dead run for the final half of the leg.

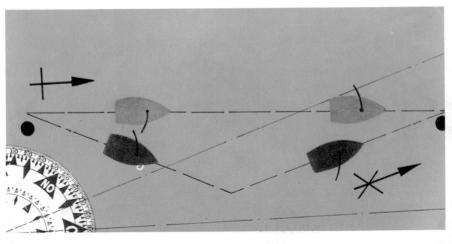

Chapter 7.
TUNING
AFLOAT

Jib fairlead position

It is not possible to tune the boat accurately ashore. Many small adjustments can only be made afloat under actual sailing conditions, where movement, heeling and changes in apparent wind bring in new factors affecting mast bend and sail sheeting tensions.

The jib fairlead position is critical to windward performance. If it is too far aft (see upper pair of photographs) then the leach will be too free and the slot will be wider than necessary. The sail will not be able to develop enough power in these light conditions and pointing will be poor.

If pointing is good but the speed is low and there is also a great deal of back-winding of the luff of the mainsail then the jib leach is too tight. If the sail is otherwise of good shape then the fairlead is too far forward. In the centre photographs it can be seen that the leach is pulled nearly into a straight line.

A rough guide to the correct position is to look from outside the lee quarter of the boat to see if the leach curve is a close match to the curve of the mainsail in the area of the slot (see lower photographs).

The aim is to get the slot as narrow as possible without too much

tension on the jib leach or too much backwinding in the mainsail. Arrange for the most frequently used fairlead positions to be near the centre of the range of possible adjustments.

Athwartships adjustment

Some means of adjusting the angle of attack of the jib is needed so that a wider angle is used for heavier winds to widen the slot, give more forward power and help with holding the boat upright.

In light winds a greater jib camber and higher pointing angle can be obtained by moving the fairlead inboard. In order to match the curve of the slot it is usually also necessary to move it forward and at the same time to ease the sheet. (See the photographs above).

The foresail leach

In practice, when sailing to windward, it is more important to get the leach area of the jib correct, and its relationship to the slot, than almost anything else. Not only can the actual cut of the sail help or hinder the vital action of the slot but the proportion of sheet tension which is transferred to the leach can also improve it or ruin it.

When tuning afloat the cut of the sail cannot be altered, but adjustments to the fairlead and its affect on leach tension can make all the difference to performance in varying wind strengths. In a squall the fairleads can come aft thus easing leach tension, widening the slot and making the boat easier to hold upright. The pointing angle will not be so good but, to compensate for this, boat-speed will be greater.

In a lull one needs the fairlead further forward transferring a greater proportion of the sheet tension to the leach to build up maximum driving force and this also enables the boat to point higher. The crew can hold up this increased force in the lighter wind and so boat-speed will still be good.

Heavy-wind jibs should be cut slightly hollow on the leach to prevent any tendency for the edge to curl in.

Right
A close-hauled Flying Dutchman in a heavy wind. The loose genoa leach and open slot perfectly suit these conditions.

The genoa leach

A genoa overlaps the mainsail by a large amount and so all the effects previously discussed are greatly magnified.

A useful way of adjusting the leach tension when close-hauled is by altering the genoa halyard by means of a multiple purchase on the mast. (See pages 22 and 57.) This acts on the mast rake, but of course the forestay must be slack to achieve any result. In heavy winds it is better to ease the halyard rather than the tack tackle since the latter raises the foot and opens the gap between foot and deck which allows air to escape. Fairlead adjustment in both directions is also effective but not so easy to arrange as it is on boats with smaller foresails.

The mainsheet traveller

The mainsheet traveller has become an essential part of the modern racing yacht, but its undoubted value is only realised if it works perfectly in all conditions. This means that it must run freely on a rigid track under the very heavy loading that it is likely to experience in strong winds. The best types run on wheels with properly engineered bearings or on a re-circulating ball-race.

The traveller should be controlled by lines which are smooth running and not too thin, so that its position and limits of travel can be adjusted easily and quickly. Stops, pins or spring-loaded plungers are of little practical value.

In light weather when close-hauled the traveller is brought to the centre of the boat, or even up to windward, so that the mainsail can be sheeted close enough without too much leach tension. Then the boat can point high and, even though the jib is also closely sheeted, there will be little backwinding effect. This technique can be over-done however. A point is eventually reached when the sail stalls (see photograph, left and also page 49).

In medium and heavy winds one can hold the traveller control in the hand and it is often far more effective to play this in the varying gusts than the mainsheet itself.

Letting the traveller go to lee-ward frees off the sail leach without letting the sail twist too much and allow the mast to bend. This is exactly what is needed when a gust strikes. (See photograph, right.)

When the gust eases the traveller is brought more central, the mast straightens and the power of the sail is restored.

If, on the other hand, the main-sheet is eased in a gust the mast straightens and the sail becomes fuller, which is the opposite to what is required. On a close reach the relative difference is greater and at all times it is much easier and faster to use the traveller method.

An example of time saving occurs on approaching the lee mark. The traveller is right out and the sheet mostly pulled in. It is only necessary on rounding to pull in the traveller in one movement. Half the sheet is already in on the new tack and the remainder of the sheet can be adjusted at comparative leisure afterwards.

Similarly, when gybing from a run to a reach, one first sets the traveller to leeward and pulls the mainsheet in slightly. Then adjust the lee side control line so that, after gybing, the traveller only goes to the centre line. The mainsail will need no attention during the gybe since it will be automatically sheeted approximately correctly for the new reaching course. This technique is of the utmost value when all the crews' attention is needed in gybing and resetting the spinnaker.

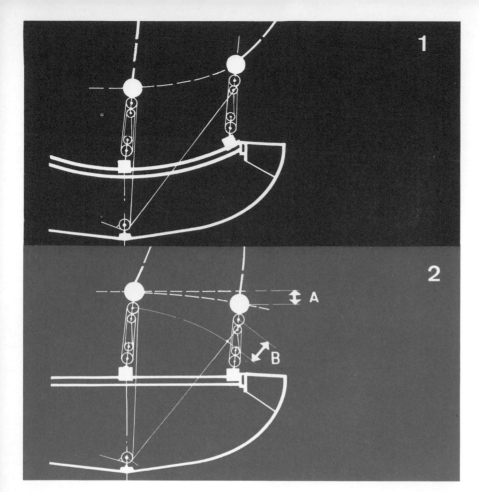

Illustration No. 2 shows a straight track which usually works better in practice. If the traveller moves from the centre to the lee side the sheet tightens automatically by the amount B. As a consequence the boom will move nearer the traveller by a fifth of this amount, A (with a four-part mainsheet purchase plus a hauling part), the sail will be flattened and the mast will bend more which is just what is needed when a gust strikes.

Conversely the sail will be made fuller automatically when the traveller is pulled in without any other attention from the sheet.

A convex track can be used to obtain a greater effect. Different numbers of parts in the mainsheet system and different arrangements of the lead blocks can also be used to adjust its effectiveness.

A more marked action is required in boats where the traveller is a long way from the mast and a finer adjustment where the distance of travel is very small—for example in a Soling.

If the traveller control is to be played in the manner just described, some thought must be given to the way the track is set up. It does not have to be straight. It can be concave or even convex.

With a concave track arranged as in illustration No. 1, and with a sheeting system using a swivelling floor block for the final lead, the sheet will tighten as the traveller moves to lee. But the traveller also rises, and, since there are four parts in the mainsheet purchase the boom will, in this example, rise by a larger amount than it is lowered by the the tightening of the sheet. Thus the sail leach tension will be eased and the mast will straighten.

Similarly, on pulling the traveller in when there is a lull in the wind, the sail will be flattened and both these effects are the opposite to what is needed. The mainsheet will require adjustment each time the traveller is moved and this is inefficient and wastes time.

The cunningham hole

If tension is put on the bias direction of a piece of cloth, it stretches and at the same time draws material from the middle of the cloth towards the line of tension. This principle is used on a mainsail by pulling the luff tighter with a line connected to the cunningham hole near the tack.

The camber in the sail is thus pulled nearer the luff, while the leach area is consequently made flatter.

In the photographs the boat on the left has the Cunningham loose. On the right the Cunningham is tight which has flattened the sail.

The same system can be used on a jib or genoa where it is particularly useful, since mast-bending is not possible and this is the only effective way of adjusting the camber for varying wind strengths. (See also pages 27 and 73).

The practical use of the cunningham control is not simply a matter of pulling it tight or of letting it go. The system used must provide for an infinite range of variations between these extremes. The exact needs of the rig can only be decided by the feel of the boat and the look of the sail, and this takes experience.

The state of the cloth just behind the luff gives a good general guide however. When the sail is full of wind horizontal folds indicate too little tension (photograph, left).

Vertical folds indicate too much tension (photograph, right).

Another rule is that off-wind, and if the boat can be held upright, less cunningham tension is needed than for a close-hauled sail. A boat running needs no extra sail luff tension except in very strong winds.

Left: Cunningham too loose.

Right: Cunningham too tight.

Mainsail foot tension

Do not neglect the clew outhaul position. Though this is not quite so important as luff tension, a proper control which can be adjusted under way should be fitted to any racing boat.

Do not make the common mistake of always setting the sail right on the maximum limit (black band). In heavy winds the foot should be tight but in lighter winds this will flatten the camber in the lower part of the sail too much.

The general rule for setting the foot tension is the same as for the luff, but turned 90°. Vertical folds mean that the foot is too loose (photograph, left). Horizontal folds mean that it is too tight (photograph, right).

Take care not to pull the clew out beyond the measurement limit mark (photograph, right).

Left: Foot tension too loose.

Right: Foot tension too tight.

For spinnaker sheets choose the lightest available line since too much weight, especially in light airs, can prevent the spinnaker from setting properly.

Watch out for the following points when choosing sheet rope:
*Is it flexible enough?
*Is it as light as possible?
*Does it resist kinking?
*A hard smooth surface may slip through cleats.
*Is a floating type suitable?
*Think again if a thinner rope would do.

For a really smooth-working sheeting system use large diameter, low-friction blocks or ball bearing blocks.

The worst and most common fault in trimming sails is to sheet in too hard (see photograph, above). This is particularly true of the mainsail. The helmsman imagines he is pointing very high and this is reinforced by the weather helm that it produces. The sail looks smooth and perfectly set but the speed is disappointing with no obvious cause.

Sail sheeting

When thinking about sail sheeting the actual material and construction of the sheets themselves should come first. Avoid thick rope which holds a great deal of water and adds appreciably to the all-up weight of the boat. Thick ropes will not run freely through standard blocks and give greater resistance to over-hauling in light airs.

The only disadvantage to thin sheet rope is that it is hard on the hands, but this can be avoided by the use of special sailing gloves which are now available.

Better still are the tapered sheets in which the part which runs through the blocks when close-hauled or close-reaching is very thin, whilst the part held in the hands is soft and thick. The two parts are sewn together with a tapered joint. There is also a slight benefit in reduced wind resistance. (See page 14)

The mainsheet should be eased until there is just a little backwinding near the mast. At this point we say that the sail is just lifting or luffing.

Another very common error is to sheet in the jib too hard and too fast immediately after tacking and before the boat has regained speed. The apparent wind is more aft at this moment and the jib has to be sheeted in smoothly and steadily as it moves forward and the speed picks up.

The sheet needs gentle and sensitive treatment to avoid the sail stalling. If this does happen it must be eased until smooth air-flow is re-established before the speed building process can be re-started.

The mainsheet also needs attention on tacking. It should be eased slightly and then gradually hardened in sympathy with the jib as the speed builds up.

Exactly the same thing occurs at the start. On gun-fire most helmsmen sheet in hard immediately, whereas they should give the speed a chance to build up first. Even worse is the common practice at a windward start of reaching down the line with sheets pinned in the mistaken belief that time will be saved when comming hard on the wind at the gun. It takes a surprisingly long time for the air-flow to become re-established over such a stalled air-foil.

It is much better to move ahead slowly with fluttering sails and then to sheet in steadily at the gun. The sails will not become stalled and optimum air-flow will establish itself immediately.

An often involuntary fault seen on boats with large genoas such as Flying Dutchmen is an oversheeted mainsail with a genoa not sheeted in hard enough. The reason is simply the mechanical difficulty of getting this large genoa sheeted tight with a single line whereas the mainsail has a multi-part purchase of great power. The result is too much weather helm with the rudder acting as a brake and with poor pointing ability (see photograph above).

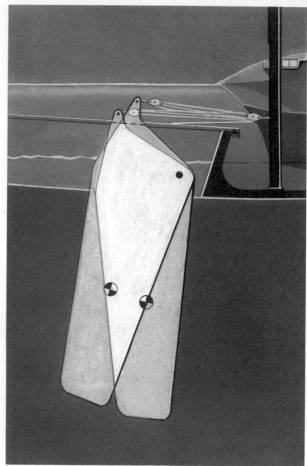

Adjustment of the centreboard

On the left drawing the Centre of Effort of the sail plan is marked (blue/green dots) and is compared with the Centre of Lateral Resistance of the hull, centreboard and rudder combined, with the centreboard down (red dots) and also with the centreboard partly raised (black dots). To give a balanced helm when sailing close-hauled the C of E of the sail should be a little ahead of the CLR and further ahead in stronger winds.

It is often possible to move the centreboard pivot fore and aft. If the boat has too much weather helm in windward trim then the pivot can be moved more aft, and vice versa.

Raising the board slightly can deal effectively with a case of weather helm, and this method is especially useful if the wind increases temporarily during a squall. There are some classes in which the pivot position has to be fixed and this then is the only solution and in any case it is much more effective to rake the board.

The drawing on the right shows this clearly. The centre of area of the centreboard is marked and it can be seen how much it moves aft when the centreboard is raised only slightly. The total area is hardly reduced at all and hence leeway remains the same.

Weather helm

Factors which affect balance are many and they often act in combination. There are many possible causes of excessive weather helm in windward sailing and there is no simple answer to the problem. One can, however, list all the main causes which can be checked one at a time.

1   Mast too far aft (But see also page 68)
2   Mainsheet too tight.
3   Mast too stiff.
4   Slot between foresail and mainsail too restricted.
5   Mainsail leach too tight or closed.
6   Genoa leach too tight or hooked.
7   Traveller is too far to windward.
8   Too little backstay tension.
9   Too much pressure on mast control at the deck.
10 Centreboard is too far forward.
11 Centreboard is pivoted too vertical.
12 Rudder blade is angled aft too much.
13 Boat is heeling too much.
14 Boat is trimmed too much down by the bow.
15 Not enough cunningham tension on the mainsail.

Since there are so many individual causes there are enormous numbers of possible combinations, but often one can arrive at a single basic cause.

For example, if the mast control is too rigid, then the mast will be too stiff and this in turn can cause the slot to be restricted, and it also makes the mainsail too full, and hence too much closed on the leach.

So this gives four combined factors all contributing to weather helm, but the basic cause is the mast control. Easing this off will also effect the other three faults. It may not completely correct them because, for example, the mainsail may still be basically too full, in which case it remains for this to be dealt with (see pages 32 and 88).

So it saves a great deal of trouble if the basic cause is found first.

Lee helm

This effect is not so common but when it occurs it can be ruinous to performance.

Weather helm gives a certain amount of braking effect, but the boat is still easy to steer at the best angle to the wind, whilst tacking is semi-automatic. A boat with lee helm is very difficult to keep on the wind, however, and tacking, especially in strong winds, is difficult if not impossible.

To eliminate lee helm one should check on the same factors listed under 'Weather helm' remembering that the causes will be in reverse.

In many classes the centreboard is only fully lowered in light weather, whereas in heavy winds the balance is greatly improved by raising the board.

Sailing upright in heavy winds

If a boat is allowed to heel, leeway increases and so does the forward resistance of the hull. Sailing a boat upright in heavy winds is particularly important and it is also particularly difficult in these conditions. The crew on the trapeze and the helmsman hiking out provide practically the only counter force to balance the power of the wind acting on the rig, and this force is at a maximum when the boat is dead upright. Once the boat is allowed to heel the leverage is reduced.

The photographs above show, on the left a badly trimmed boat; on the right, a well trimmed boat.

Looked at another way one could say that the crew should be fully extended whilst there is enough wind acting on the rig, to carry them. If they can hold the boat level in a fresh wind without being fully extended then the rig is not developing maximum power.

Classes vary and it is not possible to give exact instructions on adjusting the trim to these requirements. Some of the possibilities which are open to owners of one type of boat are not available to others and so, as before, we have listed a number of points which ought to be checked if a crew is having difficulty in holding their boat level. The answers may be a combination of several separate things acting together and so it is necessary to analyse your findings.

Kicking strap (or boom vang)

The primary task of the kicking strap is to hold the boom down when reaching and running so that the air-foil of the sail is relatively untwisted. This means that maximum sail power is developed, the sail has the greatest projected area when the wind is aft, and also the tendency to rolling is reduced.

Another important use, in conjunction with the other rigging, is to pre-set the amount of fore and aft mast bend and hence adjust the power of the mainsail.

In a top-class boat it must be possible to adjust the kicking strap tension whilst the crew is hiked out, and so the efficiency of the gear and the way it is laid out should be carefully designed with this in mind. Look also at the lower anchorage point and its relationship to the gooseneck swivel. If it is aft of this point then the kicking strap tension will increase as the boom swings outboard. This means in practice that the anchorage should be as low as possible on the mast itself and not on the hull.

1   Helmsman and crew can use heavy weight clothing. (Up to 20 kgs—44 lbs—under new rules)
2   Use flatter, less powerful sails.
3   Increase mast-bend fore and aft (see also page 25).
4   Increase mast-bend sideways (see also pages 23 and 24).
5   Decrease genoa leach tension by easing halyard (more aft mast rake), or by moving the fairlead aft.
6   Widen the slot between mainsail and jib leach by moving the fairlead outboard.
7   Tighten the cunningham control on the mainsail and/or the foresail.
8   Let the mainsheet traveller go more to leeward.
9   Raise the centreboard a little.

Finally, the helmsman should pay great attention to his steering. By watching to windward he should luff slightly before a puff strikes. Correctly done, this can have a big effect on maintaining the best upright trim.

Chapter 8.
SAILING TO
WINDWARD

Windward ability

When discussing the windward ability of a boat it is necessary to distinguish between the angle to the wind that the boat is heading (pointing angle) and the angle between the wind and the actual track of the boat including leeway (course-made-good). The boat travels slightly crabwise through the water. The difference between these two directions is the angle of drift, or leeway.

In the series of photographs on the left the boat's leeway is quite obvious. It can be seen that the boat is pointing to the left (windward) of the camera axis and yet its actual course takes it leeward of the the camera as is shown by the position of the buoy which is, of course, fixed to the sea bottom.

Leeway can never be eliminated completely, and so one always has to take it into consideration when trying to get to windward as fast as possible. As so often happens in sailing, the best solution varies depending on the prevailing conditions, which results in a number of possibilities for the tuning and trimming of the boat.

In the following paragraphs some of the factors which can effect windward ability are discussed. Look also at the drawings on the following pages.

1 *Stiffness of the centreboard*

Flexing and twisting of the centreboard increases leeway and this effect is especially marked in puffy winds. Therefore the utmost stiffness in construction is essential for optimum windward ability.

2 *Leach area of foresail*

As discussed previously, a headsail which has draft running right to the leach enables the boat to be pointed high on the wind. A flat or free leach encourages boat-speed at the expense of the pointing angle. The camber, or draft, can be encouraged to move aft by easing the cunningham control.

3 *Athwartships position of jib fairleads*

Moving the fairleads inboard enables the boat to be pointed higher on the wind but, to avoid strangulation of the slot, the sail needs to be sheeted very carefully. In fact it is best to use a jib of special cut which is very full in the foot and in which the upper leach is flat and can twist off to leeward in the area where it is very close to the mainsail.

4 *Headsail leach tension*

Moving the fairlead forward to transfer proportionately more tension to the leach also aids pointing ability. Take care not to sheet in 'too tightly and thus close the slot too much.

5 *Mainsail leach*

A mainsail with a tight leach (or with the draft or camber well aft, which is the same thing) enables the boat to point high. The mainsail can be encouraged towards this shape by easing the cunningham and by straightening the mast both fore and aft and sideways.

6 *The traveller*

Pulling the traveller more to windward also helps in pointing higher. It can even be taken to windward of the centre line in extreme cases.

7 *Battens*

Fitting more flexible battens, especially the top full-width batten, will help pointing by increasing the draft of the sail.

8 *Mast bend*

By reducing side-bend the mainsail leach becomes more closed and hence the sail gains power. Also the slot becomes narrower (see pages 23 and 24) and these both help pointing. Reducing fore and aft bend puts more camber into the mainsail and also makes the leach more closed. The slot is also narrowed and again, all these things help the pointing angle.

9 *Centreboard*

More centreboard down means less leeway and hence windward ability will improve. If the pivot can be moved forward this adjustment could greatly help the pointing angle.

All these factors will aid the boat's pointing angle but there is also boat-speed to be considered. Some of these adjustments will cause a decrease in boat-speed and so the gain in pointing angle may be partly, or even more than that, offset by slower forward speed, giving a worse overall windward ability (see also page 114).

10 *Heeling*

The angle of heel also effects the pointing angle. A slight heel to leeward can give a strong impression of better pointing but it is quite false. The feeling probably arises because of the extra weather helm that is caused by heeling.

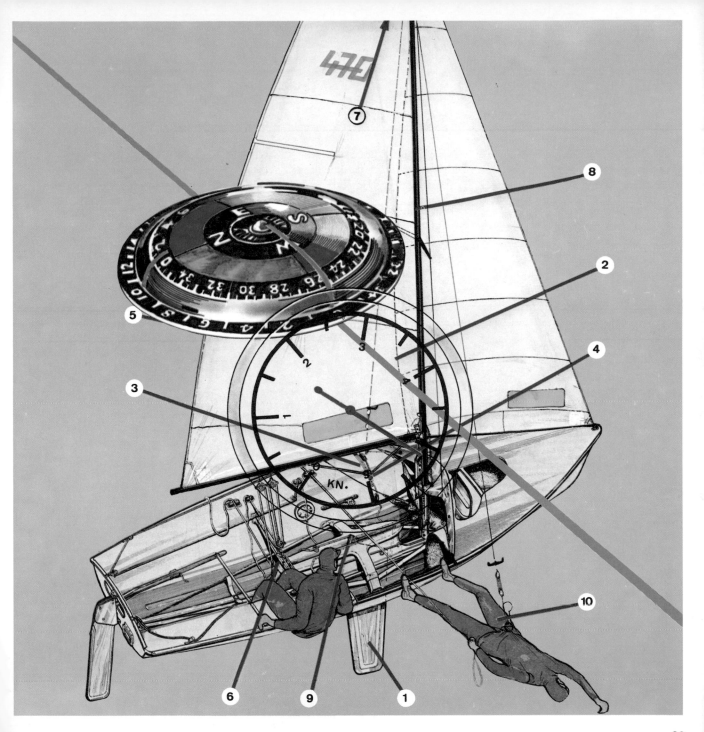

The three drawings below show a fish's eye view of a boat's hull close-hauled, the lee side being on the left.

The left-hand hull is heeling to leeward and the resulting immersed shape is asymmetric, being more bulging on the lee side and straighter on the windward side. The water has to flow faster round the lee side and this gives a force to leeward which adds to the leeway.

The opposite occurs to the hull on the right which is heeling to windward. The slight force to windward therefore reduces leeway.

The centre hull is being sailed upright and, the immersed part being symmetrical, the leeway is only countered by the anti-drift efficiency of the centreboard, together with the lateral area of the hull, with no other forces being involved.

It is better therefore to sail with the hull upright or even heeled slightly to windward.

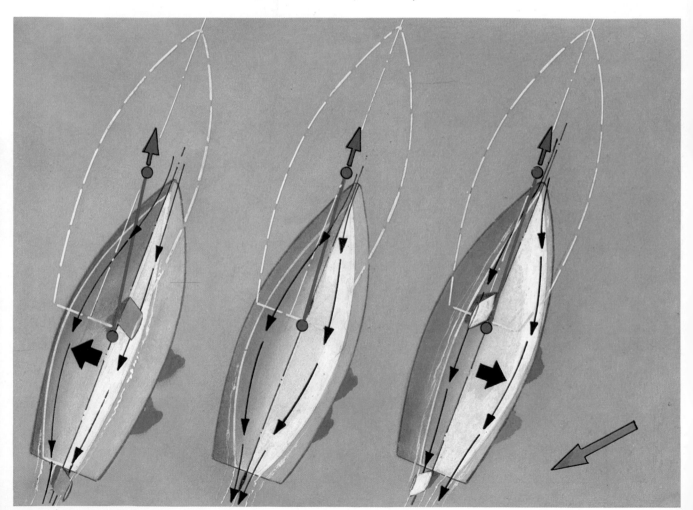

Boat-speed on the wind

On the previous pages we have emphasised the factors which improve a boat's pointing angle. On this page are listed those which can improve boat-speed to windward but some of them are only effective in fresher winds.

If, for example, your boat can point very high but the speed is poor then the following possibilities could give an improvement, though, as has been said before, pointing may suffer somewhat. A balance has to be reached between speed and pointing but some of the adjustments suggested can be made while sailing, and thus it is perfectly possible to alter the balance to suit changes in wind or waves during a race.

Thus, if you are trying to lay a mark without tacking, the traveller can be pulled to windward, the centreboard lowered fully, etc, just for those last few yards.

1 *Centreboard stiffness*
Some flexibility in the after part can improve boat-speed in gusty winds and in a short choppy sea.

2 *Foresail leach*
A free and open leach gives speed but has a bad effect on pointing. In light winds, however, the leach area should have plenty of draft always.

3 *Athwartships position of fairleads*
Moving the jib fairleads outboard directs slightly more of the sail's force in a forward direction giving an increase in speed but at the expense of pointing.

4 *Tension on the foresail leach.*
Especially in fresher winds, easing tension on the foresail leach by raking the mast aft or by moving the fairlead aft will give an increase in speed but, again, the pointing angle will suffer. A different compromise has to be found for each wind speed.

5 *Mainsail leach*
A more open, or flatter, leach will produce proportionately more forward force but less total force and hence, higher speed is obtained only in fresher winds, and also the pointing angle will suffer.

6 *The traveller*
Moving the traveller to leeward also has the effect of directing the sail's force more forward and hence can result in better speed. The total power of the sail is not reduced and so this can be effective in lighter winds if pointing is not important.

7 *Sideways mast-bend*
Side-bend has a multiple effect (see pages 23 and 24). In particular the slot widens, the jib leach is eased slightly, the mainsail leach is freed off and the pressure in the upper part of the mainsail is reduced. Pointing suffers but, in the case of a very full mainsail, it can be an advantage to bend the mast to windward in the middle to enable the bulge of the sail to clear the foresail leach more. There will then be an increase in speed without a loss in pointing.

8 *Fore and aft mast-bend*
Increasing the bend slackens the jib leach slightly and has a big flattening effect on the mainsail. So, in fresher winds, more speed results with very little deterioration in the pointing angle.

9 *Adjustment of the centreboard*
Swinging the board aft can increase boat-speed and this is especially effective in higher wind speeds. Of course, it is not possible to do this with a dagger board which cannot pivot.

10 *Heeling*
It will already be clear that the boat should be sailed upright for maximum speed. The only exception is in nearly calm conditions when a heel to leeward can decrease the hull's wetted surface area and also encourage the sails to drop into a curved airfoil shape.

Trim and steering

The steering and balance of a centreboard boat are very greatly influenced by the way the hull is trimmed. This makes it very important to counteract not only heeling but also errors in fore-and-aft trim.

A little experiment when sailing on a reach will immediately demonstrate that allowing the boat to heel to leeward gives increased weather helm. This can become very severe and the rudder will have considerable braking effect in its effort to keep the boat on course.

Heeling to windward produces

Left
The crew and helmsman of this 470 have moved forward to lift the transom until it is just touching the wake. This gives minimum drag and extra weather helm for this light wind.

equally marked lee helm which is difficult for the helmsman to counter since he has to push the tiller away at the same time as he is being tipped over backwards.

Practice is needed to sail the boat level in puffy conditions. The gusts and lulls have to be anticipated and the tiller moved in advance of the boat heeling.

Trimming the boat down by the bow also causes weather helm. In light winds it is sometimes worth accepting this in the interests of lifting the stern and reducing hull drag.

In fresh winds the weight should be moved aft to reduce weather helm by lifting the bow.

Right
This Flying Dutchman has an ideal trim for this very strong wind. Note the mast bend as well as the position of the bow. The centreboard also has been swung aft to assist in reducing weather helm and this makes the boat lively and responsive to the effects of the gusts.

A stiff mast close-hauled

This 470 has a mast which is rigged so that it is held absolutely stiff. The spreaders have been angled rather forward of the shrouds and are being pulled aft by them (see page 25). The shrouds are fully tensioned and the mast control at the deck is set up tight.

The result is a mast held rigidly straight giving maximum draft to the mainsail and suitable for light winds.

Mast bend, low down

The same 470 in the same conditions in which only one change has been made to the rig. The mast control at the deck has been eased off which has let the mast bend mainly in the area just above the deck.

The effect is to ease the jib leach and flatten the lower part of the mainsail. The boat-speed will therefore be higher. In increasing wind, when the helmsman also has to hike out fully, this is the best trim. The trim should be adjusted so that the boat can be just sailed upright with both crew fully out. If the mast control had not been eased this boat would have been impossible to hold up.

A flexible top

If the top section of the mast is made somewhat flexible, it will bend under the effects of a gust and this will free off the mainsail leach. The boat will not heel so much and will also accelerate easily in the gusts.

The middle of the mast is held stiff and so the slot remains the same, the jib leach tension is maintained and so the pointing angle also remains the same. The advantage of this type of rig is that the moment the gust eases, the mast straightens and the trim and sail-power are restored. So in puffy conditions this is a good system since it is semi-automatic and this saves time and trouble.

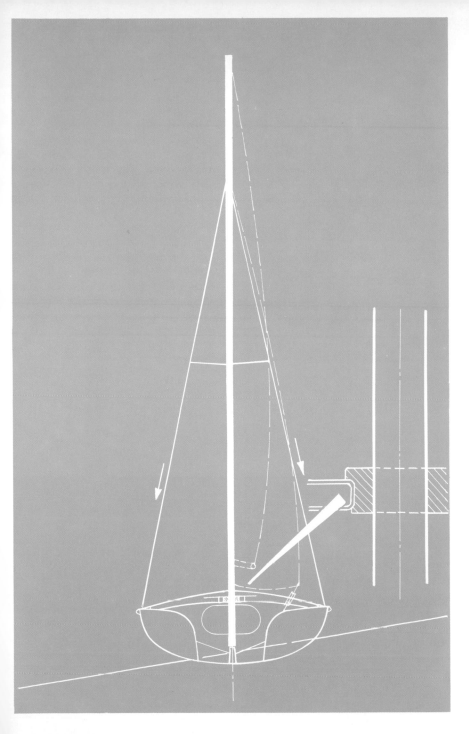

Sideways stiffness

If the mast is first rigidly chocked at the deck so that there is absolutely no sideplay, it can then be prevented from bending sideways by adjusting the spreader lengths and keeping the shrouds very tight. Then, whatever else happens, one can maintain the best possible pointing angle.

If the wind increases, the shroud tension can be eased which allows the upper part of the mast to bend off to leeward. This method is better if the wind is steady but is gradually increasing.

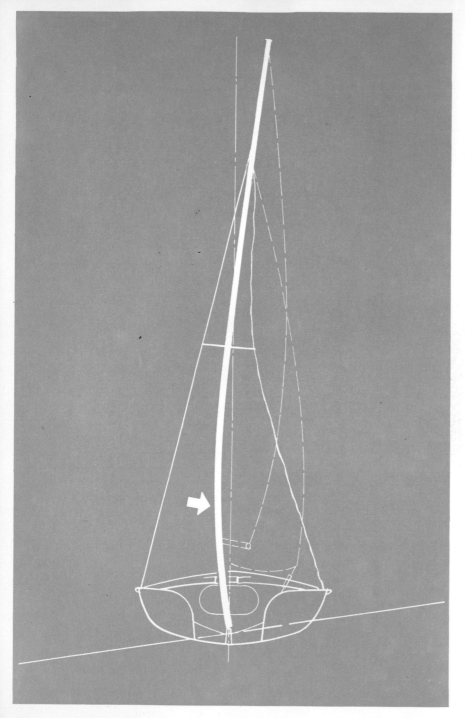

Side-bend, low down

The effect of allowing side-play in the mast-gate at deck level is to make it almost impossible to control the bending of the mast. The shroud and forestay loading causes the mast to bend under compression and this is not restrained in the lower part at the gate because a small amount of play allows a large amount of bend.

If the shroud tension is eased the mast can actually lean sideways. The foresail leach is also eased off and the slot widened especially low down where it is not particularly effective. So this is a condition which should be avoided.

Side-bend, higher up

In very light weather it is sometimes necessary to use a very full mainsail and, at the same time, to point very high with the jib fairlead well inboard and the jib leach quite tight. Unless the mast was considerably bowed to windward in the middle the slot would be too narrow and also the mainsail would be too full and so one should, in this case, allow a certain amount of side-play at the mast-gate.

In addition the spreaders should be shortened and the shroud tension reduced. The effect should be to get the widest possible slot with only a small amount of sail flattening.

This technique is also useful at the other extreme when, in very strong winds, a free jib leach and the widest possible slot is required to enable the boat to be held upright and the speed to be maintained. In all conditions in between these extremes there should be no side-play at all at the deck.

The positions of the crew

If the helmsman and crew place themselves well apart, as in the photograph, the boat will feel heavy and lifeless in its motion through the sea. The bow will not want to rise and fall but instead will smash into the waves as shown here. In addition, the total wind resistance will be higher if the crew are separated.

The helmsman and crew should concentrate their weight as much as possible making the bow and stern light so that they can easily move in sympathy with the waves. Keeping close together like this also reduces the crew's wind resistance considerably.

The correct positions for the crew and helmsman depend on the point of sailing and the speed (see also page 119). Sitting aft like this in light weather causes the stern to drag and increases the immersed hull surface area thus also increasing friction and drag.

In light weather the helmsman and crew should concentrate their weight well forward to lift the flat after sections and the transom clear of the water. The wetted surface area is further reduced by heeling the boat and this leads to the greatest possible speed.

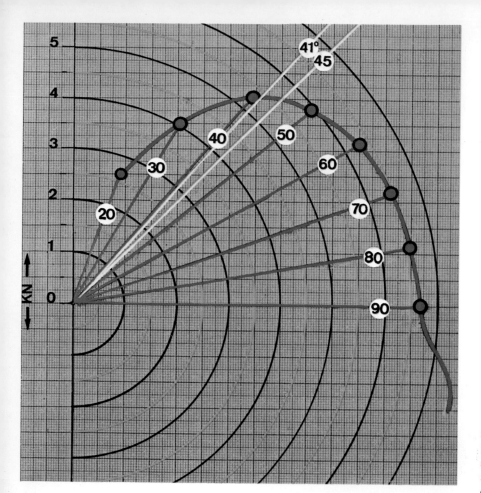

Optimum speed to windward

On previous pages we have discussed the factors which influence boat-speed and pointing angle when sailing to windward. We have seen that, in general, if pointing is improved, boat-speed will suffer and vice versa. What we have to do now is decide on the best balance to enable the speed-made-good to windward to be at a maximum. The problem is made difficult because any one type of boat needs a different solution for each set of wind and sea conditions.

The boat's speed and its angle to wind can be plotted on a graph. Here, on the left, the boat's heading is represented by the straight red lines which are drawn at the marked angles to the up and down axis which is the wind direction. Speed is shown by the alternate black and blue circles and therefore the boat-speed at any heading can be plotted and results in a curve, of which the one shown is typical. The optimum windward combination is given by the point on the red curve where it is highest above the horizontal axis. In the example shown the boat will have optimum speed-made-good to windward when it is heading between about 41° and 45° to the true wind.

Ideally, it would be possible to make such a graph for different wind speeds using an accompanying launch with accurate instruments—compass, wind speed anenometer, and a water speedometer. Then it would be easy to find the correct trim for different conditions and record the findings on the master log-sheets and the trimstrips on the boat.

Leeway is often forgotten when one tries to find the optimum trim for windward sailing. Leeway varies in a predictable way with the angle that the boat is heading with respect to the wind direction. The graph plots the angle the boat heads to the true wind against the resulting angle of leeway.

When close-hauled the boat heads between 40° and 50° to the true wind. On the graph a typical curve gives the leeway angle in this close-hauled range as lying between about 5° and 3°.

In effect, pointing closer to the wind means that the boat sails more slowly and hence the leeway angle increases. So leeway will have an appreciable effect when working out the optimum windward trim, but it is not easy in practice to find the angle accurately, since it is so small. The angles shown in the graph are typical for centreboard boats and were found after large numbers of tests under ideal conditions.

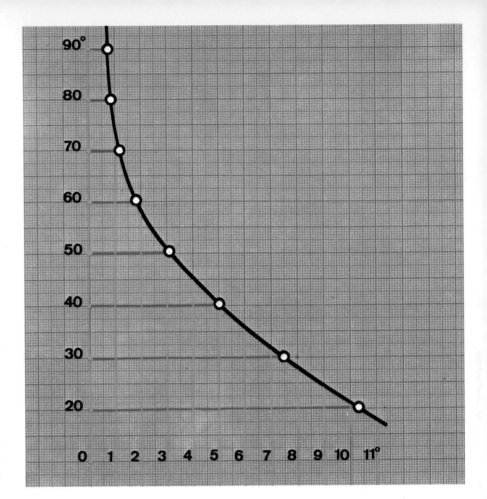

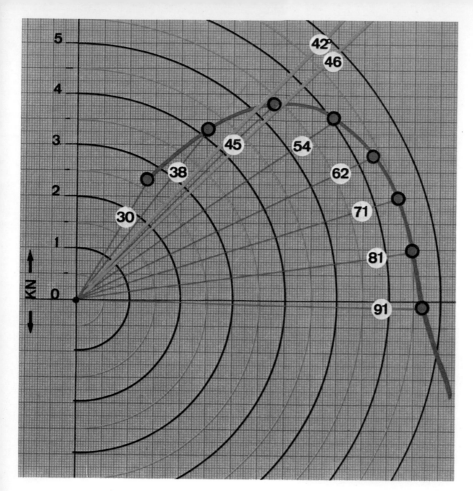

The graph on this page is similar to the previous one except that the leeway angle is added to each of the previous headings, the speed remains the same. This shows that the optimum course-made-good for best windward performance shifts to between about 42° and 46°. But to achieve this course-made-good the boat must be pointed at an angle somewhere between 38° and 42°. This is arrived at by subtracting about 4° of leeway angle from the course-made-good.

Now let us see what happens if we superimpose these two graphs.

The first graph shows the course steered in relation to the speed and gives the resulting best angle to steer. The second graph plots the course-made-good (ie adjusted to include leeway) compared with the same speeds.

From the first graph the optimum angle lies between about 41° and 45° (see yellow lines), averaging 43°.

From the second graph the optimum pointing angle lies between about 38° and 42° (see green lines), averaging 40°.

The optimum heading therefore, taking into account the leeway-angle, lies between 40° and 43°. This is the course you have to steer with respect to the true wind.

This is a rather theoretical exercise but is based on a great number of Test Reports done for the German magazine *Die Yacht* and shows clearly the difference which appears when leeway is taken into consideration. Therefore the overall windward ability of a yacht depends not only on a balance between its pointing capabilities and its speed through the water but also on its capacity for resisting leeway. This latter is a function of its hull shape and the efficiency of its centreboard and rudder.

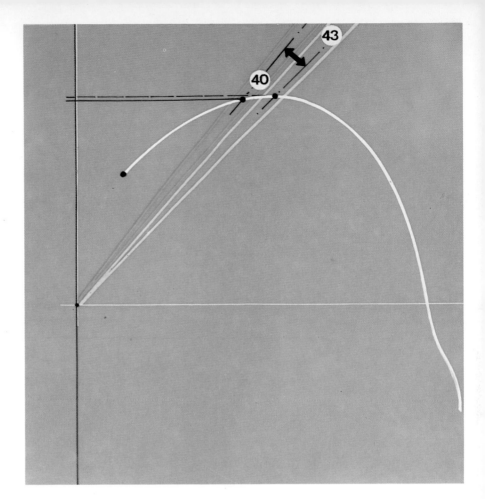

Light winds—weight forward.

High speeds—weight well aft.

Chapter 9.
SAILING ON
A REACH

As with windward sailing, so with reaching courses, there are opposing factors to consider which will effect the speed.

If the boat's performance off-wind is poor, there are a number of points which have to be checked out one by one to arrive at a solution to the problem. Several points are the same as some of those which influence close-hauled speed, but their effect is magnified when sailing off-wind because the speed is higher and the boat is perhaps able to plane.

Crew position

On page 112 the importance of where the helmsman and crew sat and its effect on speed was discussed.

In general one can say that in light weather the crew should sit well forward to lift the transom. In In medium winds they should concentrate their weights near the boat's centre of gravity. When there is a possibility of planing the crew move aft. The higher the speed the further aft they should go, the object being to put the hull into a position where it can be lifted by the water flow.

On rounding the windward mark, first raise the centreboard part way.

The centreboard

On a close or beam reach in light weather there is no advantage in raising the centreboard. The leeway is increased and speed remains about the same. If the wind increases however the needs of helm balance mean that the centreboard should be raised and, in general, the stronger the wind the more it should come up. Imbalance means too much helm has to be used so that the rudder acts as a brake preventing acceleration in the gusts and causing an increase in heeling (see page 92). Adjust the centreboard therefore until the helm is neutral when the boat is nearly upright.

In very strong winds it is best to raise the board as the boat bears away round the windward mark. The side pressure on the board is very low at this moment and it will come up easily.

The Kicking strap
(or boom vang)

This vital piece of equipment controls the mainsail shape for off-wind sailing. The object, in general, is to make the mainsail as full as possible but also the projected area must be untwisted.

Above are shown three boats with different kicking strap tension.

On the right the tension is low, the boom rises and the sail twists.

The projected area is reduced and the sail has a free and open leach with little draft.

The middle boat has the correct tension for normal conditions with the maximum possible sail camber. The leach tension is high enough to hold the sail untwisted and so the projected area is the best obtainable without bending the mast. Holding the sail steady also damps down rolling.

The left boat has so much tension that the sail is flattened on account of the mast bend. This technique is useful, however, if the boat is overpowered in heavy winds and cannot otherwise be held upright

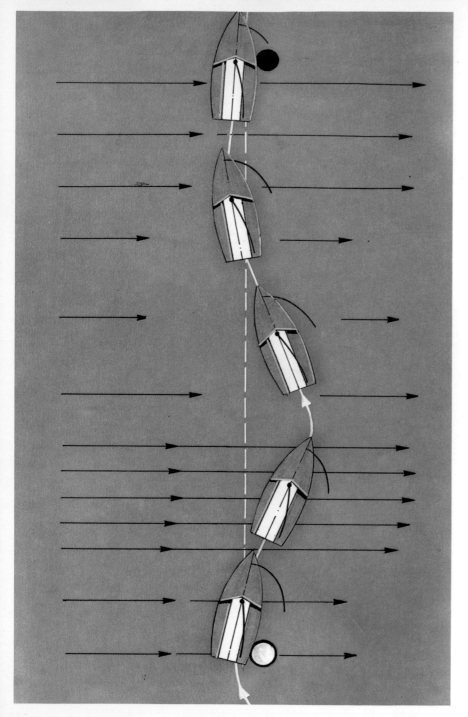

The fastest reaching course—weaving

To cover the reaching leg as fast as possible not only does one need boat-speed from correct tuning and trim, but also the best use must be made of the wind and waves. The optimum course is seldom the straight line between marks. In fact, it is only so in the unlikely event of an absolutely steady wind. Usually one can gain considerably by taking advantage of gusts and lulls.

The general rule is—bear away in the gusts and luff in the lulls.

Bearing away gives greater speed and less heeling, at the same time, the boat is travelling to some extent with the gust and therefore stays with it longer.

Luffing in the lull enables one to claw back the weather distance lost when reaching off in the gust and enables the boat to find the next gust sooner. Not only that, the closer angle to the wind may allow the crew to remain fully hiked out on the trapeze even during the lull. The speed therefore will be as high as possible.

The net result is that the distance between marks is covered considerably faster and this technique is known as weaving.

The resistance increases by the square compared with the speed and so the faster the boat the more perfect should be the hull surface (see page 3) and this is particularly important on a fast reach.

Chapter 10.
RUNNING
BEFORE
THE WIND

Crew position

As with the other points of sailing, crew position can have a significant effect on speed when running. Of course, the spinnaker is the biggest potential speed making factor, but it is so important that it is treated separately in Chapter 11, page 129.

Because there is little heeling when running the crew can move athwartships as well as fore and aft in order to give the hull the best trim on the water. The photographs show three possible crew positions which all give the same athwartships balance.

In the top picture the crew weights are concentrated and low down but, contrary to the case when beating or close-reaching, there are disadvantages to being close together on a run. The main need is to damp out rolling caused by puffy conditions or the effects of waves and you can do this better from positions further outboard where you have more leverage.

It is also much easier to handle the sheets and to see the sails from a position on the side decks and there

is an extra bonus in that the increased windage of the people actually helps when the wind is from aft.

In the lowest photograph the crew is as far as possible outboard where he has a splendid view of the spinnaker but the sheets are not so easy to handle from the trapeze. Another disadvantage of being so far outboard is the danger of either helmsman or crew touching the water which can only slow the boat. This also adversely effects their concentration.

In light weather it can be an advantage to heel the boat to windward which allows the spinnaker to drop clear of the disturbed air from the mainsail and also raises the latter higher where it can catch a better wind.

Centreboard and rudder

The centreboard should be raised almost completely in order to reduce the wetted surface area. It also helps in handling, for example, in stronger winds. Gybing should never be attempted with the board fully down since the leverage would be too great and might cause a capsize, but always leave a small part down to give some grip on the water and aid steering. Otherwise the hull will yaw and slew sideways and it will be difficult to control needing extra rudder movement which means increased resistance.

The value of the projecting tip of the centreboard in aiding control far outweighs its small extra resistance by reducing helm corrections to a minimum.

Lifting the rudder blade, on the other hand, is seldom advisable. There is a small gain in reduced wetted surface area, but it will be found that much more helm will be required and it may even be impossible to react fast enough in a luffing match or in a sudden gust.

Mast rake

The general rule is to rake the mast forward to obtain the highest speed down-wind. One reason for this is that the mainsail can be eased out further before the boom comes up against the shroud. This is very important if you have no spinnaker, in which case the shroud tension should be eased and the forestay tightened, but do not touch the jib halyard. The jib can then be ballooned out on the opposite side with greatly increased camber like a small spinnaker.

Mainsheet

The mainsheet should, of course, be eased as far as possible when running, but be sure the boom does not quite touch the shroud. Put a stopper knot in the tail of the sheet to limit it to this point. In heavy winds the boom could otherwise press on the shroud and lever the middle of the mast aft via the gooseneck. The forward pull of the spinnaker on the top part of the mainsail could then easily cause the spinnaker to collapse.

In hard gusts the mainsail is bound to twist somewhat and this will start a violent roll. It can be stopped quickly by pulling in the mainsheet a few inches.

Kicking strap (or boom vang)

The tension can be the same as for reaching courses, the object being maximum projected area and a minimum of twist (see page 121).

Optimum course down-wind

It does not always pay to steer directly before the wind and so, if the lee mark is exactly downwind you should normally aim off to one side a little and gybe back again when half way.

The principle is that the boat travels faster on a reach than on a run. The increase in speed obtained by aiming off can more than compensate for the extra distance sailed. The question is how far to aim off and this varies with the wind strength. The effect is more marked in very light winds when the hull speed is very much below its theoretical maximum and can increase dramatically when reaching. It becomes less marked as the wind speed increases until it is hardly worthwhile sailing out of the direct line in very strong winds.

The other general rule is that faster boats can profit by aiming off more than slower boats. A Tornado catamaran, for example, would gain by using this technique even in strong winds, whereas a small singlesailed dinghy like a Finn or OK would almost always sail the straight line course.

The diagrams show this principle for various types of boats in light winds (upper) and medium winds (lower). The numbers refer to (1) Tornado, (2) Flying Dutchman, (3) Tempest, (4) Soling, (5) 470, (6) Finn. The angles are arbitrary and not intended to be accurate.

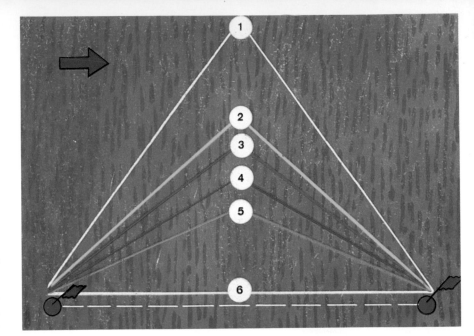

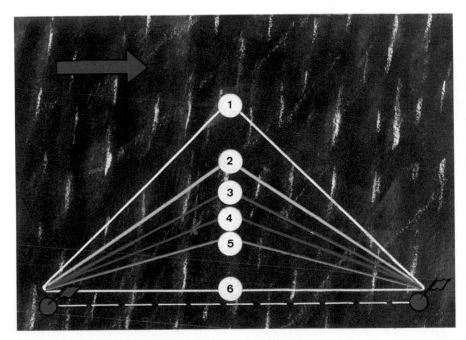

Chapter 11.
THE SPINNAKER

Height of spinnaker pole

The spinnaker is actually designed to set correctly with the tack and clew about level. The clew cannot be controlled for height since it finds its own level depending on the wind strength and the sheeting angle. Hence it is essential to be able to adjust the pole height.

The top illustration shows a pole set too high. The sail is assymmetric and causes the luff to be loose and so fall forward. In light airs it is impossible to prevent it from collapsing.

In the centre drawing the pole is too low which tightens the luff putting a greater camber on this side and unbalancing the airflow. The luff cannot be trimmed accurately and is prone to sudden collapse. The sail is not working at maximum power.

At the bottom, the tack and clew are level, the sail is easy to set and trim, and the designed shape is achieved.

In light airs the clew drops lower because the wind force cannot support the weight of the sail and the pole must be lowered.

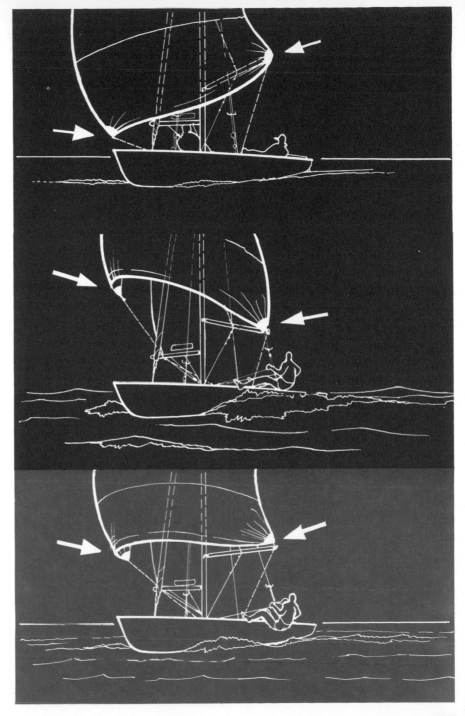

In more wind the sail flies higher and so the pole must go up. The effective limit to this is when the head of the sail flies out horizontal to the halyard sheave (see photos, right and also page 131).

In practically every class the spinnaker pole has a maximum length limit. It is always made to this size, but to gain most advantage it should be set so that it is perpendicular to the mast. This is particularly important on a reach when the sail needs to be as far forward as possible to enable it to work clear of the foresail.

Some masts have the pole attachment on a slide so that one can adjust the level. Others use a series of fixed eye-plates for the pole to hook onto.

There are classes in which only one eye-plate position is allowed and and then you are only able either to have maximum projection, or to adjust the angle to get the tack and clew level, but not both. The latter is usually the more important.

The head of the spinnaker

In the photographs on Page 131 the top of the spinnaker is shown in three different attitudes.

Above, the head is flying too high. This could be because of a wrong basic shape but also could be caused by the pole being set too high for this wind strength.

Centre, the head is drooping too low. Again the shape could be wrong or the pole could be too low. In light airs it is important for the sheets and also their clips to be as light as possible.

Bottom, when correctly set, the tangent to the curve of the sail at the head should be about horizontal. It is not possible to see this from inside your own boat. Take a trip in a launch whilst your crew alters the sheet and the pole height and see just what happens to the sail.

If set correctly, you lose nothing and can gain a worthwhile bonus in reduced turbulence and interference, by not hoisting the sail close up. Leave about a foot clear between the head swivel and the mast. However, in nearly calm conditions, when the sail is drooping, and in very strong winds when sideways swaying needs to be restricted, you should hoist it close up.

Spinnaker sheeting

Normally the spinnaker should be sheeted from a point as far aft as possible. This gives the minimum downward pull on the leaches and allows them to fly free. The only exception to this is when running in very strong winds when a more forward sheeting point gives better control to prevent the boat rolling.

A sheeting position well aft and also outboard is needed when close-reaching to enable the leach to be carried as clear of the mainsail as possible. A free spinnaker leach is vital on a close-reach because of the great quantity of air that has to be passed to leeward. A forward sheeting position curls in the leach and backwinds the mainsail, also causing extra heeling and even broaching.

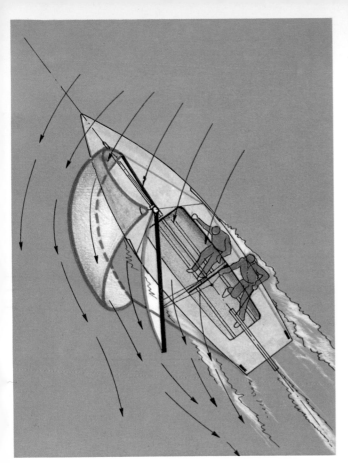
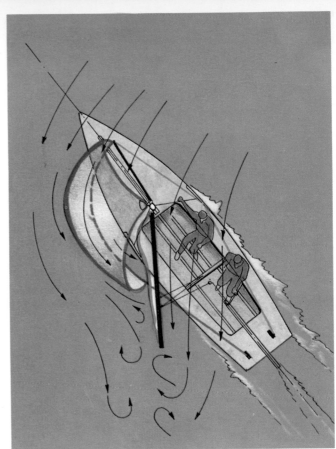

The spinnaker pole uphaul and downhaul

The pole should be held as rigidly as possible in the required position. Fore and aft it is controlled by the guy, or brace. Vertically it is controlled by the uphaul, or topping lift, and the downhaul, or vang. The particular method chosen must allow for quick setting up and quick adjustment with positive control and the one shown here does this effectively.

Stretch in the system has to be avoided and so does undue windage. Therefore the best choice could be a fine steel wire arranged as in the drawing. At the top it is fixed to the mast and where it passes through the sheave at the mast heel (1) is a stopper ferrule which is positioned so that, when the pole is set the ferrule is hard up against the sheave.

Adjustment for height is provided at the cleat on the pole. Slip is prevented by the ferrules on the wire.

When the pole is removed, the wire (2) is pulled in by the shock cord (3) and lies tightly against the mast.

This system is very effective for small boats, the only disadvantage being that the loose guy method of setting the spinnaker is not feasible. For this the downhaul must pass through the deck a few inches ahead of the mast to hold the pole forward.

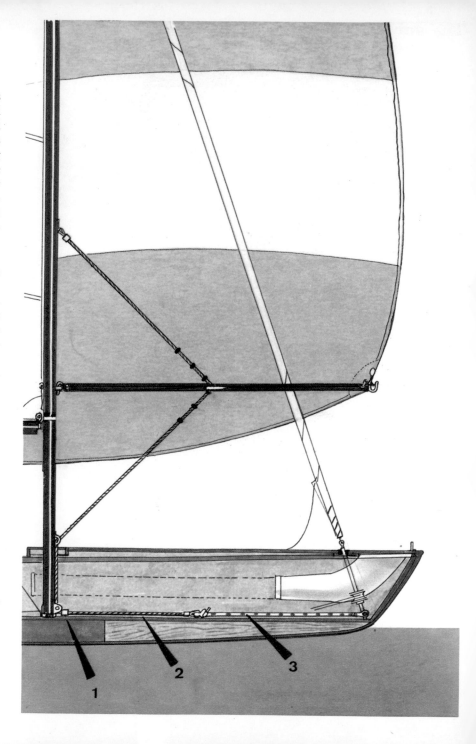

The spinnaker sheets

The need is for the lightest possible sheets which are also thin and yet can still be handled. Light—to avoid weighing down the leach and strangling the exit for the air. Fine—to allow them to run out freely and with minimum friction

In strong winds it is better to use thin sheets and wear gloves than to change to thicker lines.

The sheets should be marked so that they can be set to the correct positions before gybing, especially onto a reach. A good guide for this is put a distinctive mark on the sheet near the cleat when the pole is just touching the forestay. Just before gybing the old sheet is cleated and when, after gybing, it becomes the new guy, it is exactly correctly set.

Different coloured marks are used for gybing on a run where the pole is set further aft.

Sheets of a distinctive colour are also a help to avoid confusion with other small sized control lines and it is best to make the sheet and guy from one continuous line so that the end can never be lost.

Close reaching under spinnaker

How close a spinnaker can be carried effectively does not depend on whether one can still keep it full of wind, but whether the speed is increased when it is set. The cut of the sail is the deciding factor and so each sail should be tried out in different conditions and the results noted.

In general, if the mainsail has to be sheeted hard in to prevent excessive backwinding, then the spinnaker should be dropped even though it may be still full of wind (see photograph).

In fresh winds when running it always pays to carry the spinnaker provided the crew are capable of managing it. The speed will always be less with a boomed out foresail alone. Even keel-boats, travelling at maximum displacment speed will nevertheless gain in the lulls that always occur even in the strongest winds if they have a spinnaker set and there may also be the chance of surfing on the face of a wave.

Right

This spinnaker is just on the point of 'breaking'. A stable spinnaker will not collapse until a considerable amount of the luff has folded back giving plenty of time to adjust the trim.

Trimming the spinnaker

There is no mystery or black magic in setting and trimming a spinnaker perfectly. It is not an art that you are born with, as some people say. It is something which can be learnt very easily and, like anything else, practice makes perfect.

The spinnaker demands constant and unflagging attention. To get maximum power from the sail the sheet has to be constantly eased to the point where the luff is starting to curl in (see photograph). This critical point is just before it collapses and therefore the crew is making continuous small sheet adjustments and never takes his eyes off the luff. To enable him to see clearly what is happening the cloth should be of contrasting colours in this area.

It is easy to keep the spinnaker quiet by pulling in the sheet a little. The sail looks nice and is always full of wind, but appearances are deceptive. A far more effective driving force is obtained when it is held just on the point of 'breaking'.

Dealing with gusts

The wind is never constant and the spinnaker is a large and powerful sail. Therefore its correct trimming, so that it is always just on the point of breaking, can give a huge advantage over competitors whose spinnaker work is not quite perfect.

The diagram shows what happens when the boat sails into a gust. The orange arrow is the true wind. The dark blue arrow is the wind created by forward motion of the boat. Arrow (1) therefore shows the apparent wind as felt on board. This is the wind to which you have to trim the spinnaker. When a gust strikes the true wind increases. This is the yellow arrow. The boat's speed at this moment is the same (dark blue arrow, and the apparent wind jumps to (2), which is slightly more aft. So the first trimming action is to ease the sheet slightly

Boat-speed will however increase due to the gust and so the boat's own-wind also increases (light blue arrow). This causes the apparent wind to shift forward (3) and the sheet has to be trimmed in.

When the gust passes (orange arrow) the boat will continue for a moment at the previous high speed with the resulting high own-wind speed (light blue). Thus the apparent wind shifts forward even more and the sheet has to come in even more.

Finally the speed drops and we return to position (1) which requires the sheet to be eased again.

So a summary of the trimming

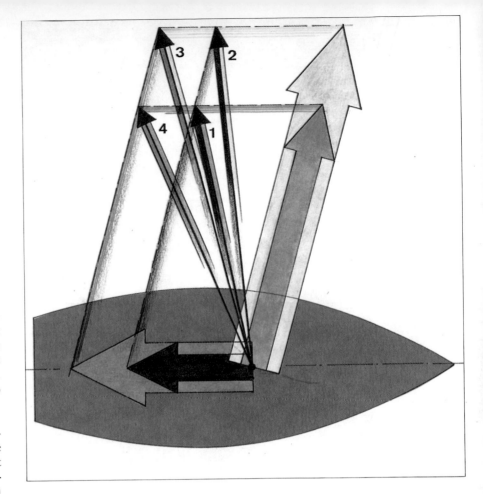

movements for the passage of a gust is as follows:

    *Ease out briefly (2)

    *Trim in while the gust lasts (3)

    *Trim in briefly (4)

    *Ease out as the speed drops (1)

These trimming movements can be modified when the crew and helmsman learn to work together so that the boat is made to bear away slightly when the puff strikes and to luff when it passes (see page 122). These helm movements partly cancel the major sheet trimming actions.

In very puffy conditions it may also be necessary to ease off the guy during gusts and to recover it again afterwards.

Old and new spinnakers

An old spinnaker like that on the left should only be used in light airs. Never try to save wear and tear on a new spinnaker by using the old one only in strong winds. The old sail will blow out of shape and be useless (see page 40).

A new spinnaker is often too loose on the leaches and hence is too flat. Therefore use it in heavy winds first where it will give minimum back-wind to the mainsail and the boat will be easy to hold upright. Notice how the 'ears' of the sail on the right are sticking out and the whole sail in this area is too flat.

Chapter 12.
THE TRAPEZE

To make the best use of the trapeze the hooking system should be simple and sure. It is essential that hooking on can be done with one hand so that the other is free for the sheet. The hook must therefore hold itself out rigidly from the harness.

The photograph top, left shows a poor arrangement that needs two hands, one to lift up the hook, and the other to bring the wire towards it. This dangling hook could also get caught on something in the boat at a vital moment.

This belt is also very poor. It gives no support to the shoulders, is too high and the load is concentrated over the kidneys. Standing out in this belt will be very painful and could cause permanent physical damage.

Above, right and centre, left is shown a good trapeze harness. Notice the hook held firmly on a metal plate; the belt which is built into a wide back support; straps to support the shoulders; the crutch strap to position the belt and hook securely; and the adjustable fasteners to the straps.

The photographs at centre, right and below show a typical trapeze wire with its two-position ring and its handle. The height of

the ring can be set by adjusting the stop on the line which passes through the block. The clip fastens to a long shock-cord which pulls the wire tight when the crew is unhooked. This system is simple and has a low wind resistance which is important since it hangs in the airflow through the slot.

A variable height system can be fitted with a small tackle inserted between the ring and the wire but, though it is an advantage when

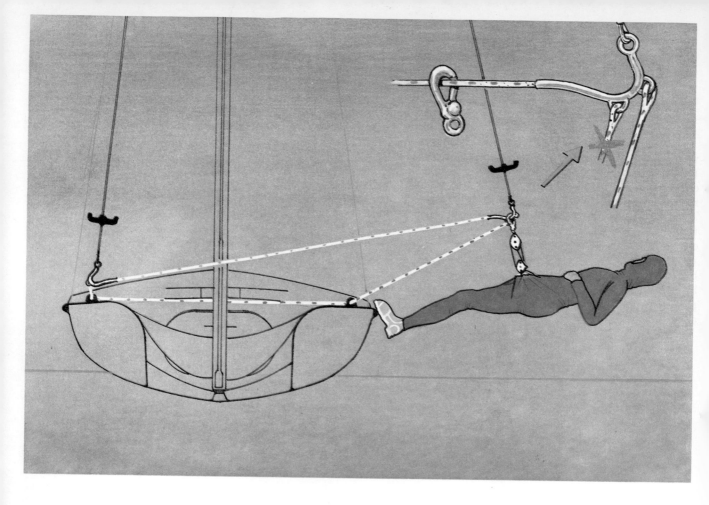

different crews have to be carried, the windage and complication is higher.

Above is a drawing of a continuous trapeze system which allows the crew to change sides without unhooking. This saves time but the gear has to be very carefully made to avoid hang-ups.

Details of the special hook-terminals are shown in the inset drawing. The hollow hooks are connected by shock cord which is fastened inside the tubes.

The snap-hook is permanently attached to a height adjusting tackle on the trapeze harness. The hook, which could also be a small block, can run on the shock cord and automatically goes onto the hook-terminal at the end. The crew has both hands free for the sheets.

The shock cord, which pulls tight the wire when not in use,

must be connected to the hook-terminal on the outside and not underneath (see inset). This cocks the hook-terminal upwards and prevents the snap-hook from sliding off accidentally.

FINAL CHECKLIST

It is essential to get out on the water well before the start of a race. In particular, sail to windward to check on the wind direction and the magnitude of rhythmic shifting. Then, about fifteen minutes before the start, make a final check to ensure that the boat's trim is exactly right for the conditions. Different boats will need a different checklist but below are given the more important checks to make on an average boat.

1. Cunningham hole tension
2. Mainsail foot tension
3. Genoa halyard tension (or mast rake)
4. Traveller setting
5. Shroud tension
6. Foresheet fairlead position
7. Is the spinnaker clear for hoisting?
8. Are the spinnaker sheets rove and free to run?
9. Are the bailers free and is the bottom dry. Bailers leak slightly and so start with them closed and with the bottom sponged out so that the weight is absolutely at a minimum.
10. Do we need lifejackets or sailing gloves?
11. Is the trapeze harness adjusted correctly?
12. Check the course.
13. Check the direction of the first mark.
14. Check which is the favoured end of the start line.
15. Decide which side of the first beat to take.
16. Check that the centreboard and rudder are clear of weed. In keelboats it is worth sailing astern for a few yards to clear weeds.
17. Check the position and angle of the centreboard and rudder.